MW01124071

Unexplained Consciousness Events:
Exploring the Possibilities

Robert De Filippis

Copyright © 2017 Robert De Filippis

ISBN: 978-1-63492-028-5

All rights reserved. No part of this publication may be reproduced, stored in a retrieval system, or transmitted in any form or by any means, electronic, mechanical, recording or otherwise, without the prior written permission of the author.

Published by BookLocker.com, Inc., St. Petersburg, Florida, U.S.A.

Printed on acid-free paper.

BookLocker.com, Inc.
2017

First Edition

Dedication

For my six beautiful grandchildren:

Sara, Matthew, Noah, Sebastian, Owen, and Jordan. May this book be one small step in the creation of a better world within which you can grow to maturity and live a good life full of love, joy, and peace.

Table of Contents

Introduction

Why read this book? Some possible reasons are:

- You've struggled with your faith tradition, want to leave but can't think of yourself as an atheist or non-believer.
- You are an atheist but have misgivings about your beliefs.
- You have strong suspicions there's more to life than we can explain.
- You want to ground your suspicions with more than hearsay and folklore.
- You have experienced a strange consciousness occurrence like a premonition of an event that happened, or communication with someone without the aid of a device, or a dream that became reality.
- You are naturally curious and want to explore the full potential of human possibilities.

These are all good reasons to take the time and make the effort to read and understand this book. I can't promise a complete transformation, but you can expect to come away with a greater appreciation for the basis of religion, the potential for the unification of science and religion as lenses on reality that don't need to be in conflict, a new understanding of your own potential and an appreciation for this planet's web of life of which we are a part.

Let's start with some astounding stories of real live people having unexplained consciousness experiences that defy understanding in what we call our common sense.

Case 1

The following quote came from Abraham Lincoln's dream journal verbatim: "There seemed to be a death-like stillness about me. Then I heard subdued sobs as if a number of people were weeping. I thought I left my bed and wandered downstairs. There the silence was broken by the same pitiful sobbing, but the mourners were invisible. I went from

1

room to room; no living person was in sight, but the same mournful sounds of distress met me as I passed along. I saw light in all the rooms; every object was familiar to me; but where were all the people who were grieving as if their hearts would break? I was puzzled and alarmed. What could be the meaning of all this? Determined to find the cause of a state of things so mysterious and so shocking, I kept on until I arrived at the East Room, which I entered. There I met with a sickening surprise. Before me was a catafalque on which rested a corpse wrapped in funeral vestments. Around it were stationed soldiers who were acting as guards; and there was a throng of people, gazing mournfully upon the corpse, whose face was covered, others weeping pitifully. 'Who is dead in the White House?' I demanded of one of the soldiers, 'The President,' was his answer; 'he was killed by an assassin.' Then came a loud burst of grief from the crowd, which woke me from my dream."

Lincoln continued to be vexed by the dream, which occurred about a week before his assassination. "Although it was only a dream, I have been strangely annoyed by it ever since," he wrote. Obviously, he anticipated his own assassination. 1

(By the way, in case you're wondering, dreaming is considered another form of consciousness.)

Case 2

A woman is awakened by a nightmare at four A.M. In it, a dear family friend has a serious medical crisis. Not wanting to wake his family, she waits until an appropriate time to call. She calls to hear her friend's wife tells her he had a massive stroke during the night. He subsequently dies.

Case 3

A lady is bedside as a dear friend is dying. Suddenly, the room fills with an intense, brilliant light. She had never experienced this kind of light in her life before. When her friend breathed her last breath, the light disappeared. The experience of this light has been reported in many other similar situations. Think of the Biblical description of Paul's experience on the road to Damascus.

Case 4

A young woman calls her father on two occasions to tell him that two of her siblings were going to be parents before they told her. She was right. Two children were born to her siblings exactly as she had predicted.

Case 5

An elderly lady living with one of her daughters tells her that her other daughter in another state is terminally ill, a fact that was being kept from her mother. Her daughter, confused about how she knew, asks how her mother came to know this. The mother tells her, "your father told me last night in a dream." Her father had died recently.

Case 6

With eyes taped shut and molded speakers inserted into her ears to emit loud clicks, the patient was fully anesthetized. The doctor opened her scalp with a unique tool to expose her brain. She had been cooled to 60 degrees F. Her brain stem showed no responses from the clicking in her ears. Her brain was in total shutdown.

After the surgery, she accurately described the 20 doctors, nurses, and technicians in the room, 17 of whom she had never met, provided a detailed description of the unique tool used to cut open her skull, and the cardiac surgeon's surprise at finding her femoral artery too small to use.

A different genre

This book falls into a genre called speculative non-fiction. The challenge involved in writing in this genre with integrity means doing four things well: 1. Stating the foundations of my topics. 2. Stating my tentative conclusions. 3. Showing the basis of these conclusions. 4. Clearly identifying my speculations.

All this is as preamble; the following section is offered for your review as you consider whether to read this book or not:

Foundation: Mechanistic universe fails to explain consciousness.

The West's model of reality is based on Newtonian physics with Einsteinian enhancements. This model says the universe is a purely material, deterministic, place where we and the objects we observe are separate and distinct. Where what happens to others has no effect on us. Where there is no meaning or purpose other than what we make of it. It says it is a cold, dead space made up of matter and energy. This model fails to explain the whole process of consciousness.

As consciousness study advances, two primary theories have emerged in contrast to each other: 1. Production theory – consciousness is produced by the brain's physiological functions. 2. Reduction theory– consciousness is universal and a primary element in the cosmos and the brain tunes in and receives only that which we need to function at this level of the universe.

Tentative Conclusions: We need a new explanation.

Being that the production theory of consciousness is understood as a purely physiological process, it fails to explain at least two certain, observable functions of consciousness: 1. The brain, a physical object, interacts with the mind, a non-physical phenomenon and vice versa. 2. Consciousness, a non-physical phenomenon, affects the outcomes of physical/scientific experiments like the classical double-slit experiment.

There must be another explanation.

Key Facts: We do not experience the universe as it is.

Cognitive science and theoretical physics tell us the universe does not function as we perceive it. We are limited by our sensory systems

4

and adapted to operate in what we call the classical 3 D level of the cosmos. We also know the most basic level the universe consists of a holistic field of probability waves where everything connects to everything else.

What appears to us as distinct and separate objects are temporal-spatial extensions of that basic fabric that last as long as the conditions that create them exist. We also know that we cannot separate the observed from the observer and by this awareness recognize that we create our own subjective experience. Some cognitive scientists have shown by mathematical calculation the speed of the brain alone is not able to create consciousness.

Certain unexplained consciousness events are not possible within the context created by the current Newtonian model.

Speculation: Unexplained consciousness events offer new clues.

A different model incorporating quantum mechanics offers us more possibilities for understanding how consciousness affects the physical level of reality.

Anecdotal accounts and formal records of unexplained consciousness events, UCE's, provide sufficient reason to believe something authentic is happening and this creates the curiosity to explore these events further. A particular category of UCE, the Near Death Experience, NDE, and the enormous body of legitimate research on same, provides the opportunity to examine human consciousness in unusual circumstances to create a fuller understanding of the entire process.

Although some NDE researchers conclude that NDE's prove the existence of the supernatural, this book proposes this is another level of this universe. If this is true, what we have called the supernatural, i.e., those experiences that seem to happen outside our normal way of understanding and explaining them, might be classified as occurring at levels of the universe we simply don't have access to from our classical 3D level.

Caveat emptor – Buyer Beware

People read for different reasons: To escape, to pass the time, to be entertained, to learn, to be transformed. This book is not light reading. It is not for the reader who wants to relax and be distracted from their daily woes. It is a book that can transform you.

It is a serious treatment of a serious topic for serious readers.

We will delve into the depths of our reality. It may be deeper than you prefer to go. And yet, here is the paradox: The deeper we go, the better we see our highest potential. At this level, we get a glimpse of our peak possibilities; we might even call it the essence of our existence.

The journey is difficult. It will take effort to absorb what you read. It will require that you re-read portions to grasp the content.

Don't buy this book if you aren't willing to put in the effort to understand it. Don't buy it if you like your explanations of the world and yourself as is. It will be a waste of your money. It's not for everyone.

But, if you read it and absorb what's here, I promise it will enhance your view of who you are and your future possibilities. It will explain how the universe provides the canvas upon which you co-create your reality. You will recognize that you are connected to everyone and everything else. You will get a glimpse of your power to have the life you want, not without limitations but certainly, more than you think you can now.

We are all integral parts of the universe, a universe of such infinitesimal and gigantic proportions we can't even apprehend, let alone comprehend its mysteries.

Some good news

My goal in writing this book is to convince the reader to question their beliefs about what's possible; to open to the possibility that we do have abilities beyond our fondest dreams.

I hope to legitimize a layperson's discussion about a topic that Western religion and science both consider their private domain of inquiry. I hope to start a conversation for possibilities.

Because it is only when ordinary people like us begin to comprehend that we are connected to and not separate from everyone else; that we are deeply dependent on this planet's web of life, of which we are a part, that positive change will begin. Until then, our futures and the futures of our children will remain in the hands of those who control the tools of destruction. These are the tools being used every day to deplete our natural resources and decimate our planet. And this all depends on a wrong-headed notion of reality.

You don't need to decide if you want to buy at this point. Read the **Free** section titled: **The Challenge of St. Paul.** When you finish, you'll know if you should spend your money.

After you've read it, you might think it's a bridge too far and decide not to buy it. If this is the case, thanks for taking the time to consider this book. I wish you the best.

On the other hand, it might stimulate your curiosity, so you'll want to read more.

Either way, thanks for considering it. For those who purchase and continue, I encourage you to contact me with questions and comments by posting them to my website, www.robertdefilippis.com.

We learn new information by adding it to existing knowledge we already possess. Think of this as a learning ladder. It's difficult if not impossible to skip the early lessons and advance to the more complex without it.

So, to assist, I've placed a note page at the end of each chapter. Use it when you finish that chapter. Hopefully, this measured approach will help in absorbing the information in each chapter that is unfamiliar to you.

Robert DeFilippis

The Challenge of St. Paul

As you begin this section, you may wonder why use St. Paul as an example of Unexplained Consciousness Events, UCE's. It's because our most hallowed ways of explaining who we are and how we function in this mysterious universe are limiting further discoveries. We've fallen victim to the treachery of a silent form of certainty in our religious and scientific ideologies. We suffer this certainty in our educational, social, cultural, business, scientific and religious systems. We depend on them to decide what is orthodoxy and what is heresy.

So, to explore another way of explaining what we consider reality. What better place to do it than religion; a firmly entrenched belief system based on tradition, ancient texts and centuries of mythology, folklore, and narrative. Let's take a closer look at Christianity: To be precise, who started it?

The danger here is you might think this book is about religion. Don't worry. It's not. The rest of the content allows us to look at how we've designed our lives to conform to predetermined models of reality. And how those models don't enable us to explain reality as it is because our subconscious narrative tells us we "already know" how it is.

What is more demonstrative of an entrenched narrative of "already knowing" than religion? Even new scientific discoveries are filtered through religious beliefs. Notice, it says "filtered" through religious beliefs. There is probably no area where people become more bound by traditional beliefs than religion. So, this chapter is an attempt to break through that rigidity to show there are entirely different ways of understanding the same phenomenon.

The topics in this book are enormous. To trim our efforts down to size, we need to have a specific tool to use for exploration. Unexplained Consciousness Events, UCE's allows us to focus our efforts. People having Near Death Experiences report events that are impossible to understand in our shared way of explaining the unexplainable, short of calling them supernatural. NDE's are a form of UCE

Don't worry if you aren't entirely clear on the details. It's only important that you know that an NDE is a type of UCE. The entire book is written to clarify any confusion that remains.

How did Christianity get started?

Surprise! Historically, Christianity was not started by Jesus? This is not a claim by a theologian. It is a historical claim. Just read the work of any legitimate New Testament *historical* scholar. (I emphasize *historical* here. You could start with Bart Ehrman or James Tabor and go from there. The bibliographies in their books will give you more resources than you can use in your lifetime.)

When and if you do read their work, it will become apparent that the only certain historical fact is that Jesus was an apocalyptic Jewish preacher who was crucified for his crimes against the Roman Empire around the year 32 of the Common Era.

He probably had twelve Jewish disciples. The stories of his death and resurrection are the basis of Christian theology. His life before his last three years is a mystery. There is no written record, factual or otherwise regarding claims of his divinity before Paul's letters were written. And divinity then was understood differently from how divinity is understood today.

Professor Ehrman's book, *How Jesus Became God, the Exaltation of a Jewish Preacher from Galilee,* offers a thorough explanation of how the concept of the divine evolved at that time.

In this book, you find that the full development of that theme, divinity, in the written record showed up twenty years after Jesus' death. It was created and propagated by a man named Saul of Tarsus after his radical conversion to become known as St. Paul.

The early Jewish sect that followed Jesus before the claim of his divinity had no reason to believe he was more than an inspired holy man with profound insights into human nature. He was a humanist, and devoted to the Jewish Torah and bringing Jews back to the law before the end times. He thought the end was at hand.

Fundamentalist Christians devoted to Christian theology will argue that the four gospels are inerrant and tell his story with integrity. But a horizontal reading of the same events in these gospels show the many irreconcilable discrepancies. They will also show how his divinity appeared in the earliest Gospel written by Mark. And then how it evolved over the next two Gospels by Matthew and Luke. Eventually leading to the last Gospel, written by John, who goes into full-throated spirituality. As Professor Ehrman writes, "from (low) exaltation to (high) incarnation divinity."

While professors know it in mainline Christian seminaries, what isn't generally understood by the faithful in the pews is that Paul's influence was more potent than Jesus' in their theology. He wrote his letters twenty years before the first gospel of Mark. So, two decades of time passed as the stories of Jesus' divinity developed.

First Mark wrote with few references to his divinity and John, 80 years later, completed the official canon with full-blown high incarnation divinity. So, in that eight decades, Jesus went from exaltation divinity, "became the son of God when resurrected," to incarnation divinity, "Jesus is God and has existed for all time."

Historically we know the canon was made official in the early 4th century some 300 years after Jesus died. During that period, dozens of documents were deemed heretical and ordered destroyed. But a few survived. An Egyptian shepherd and his grandson discovered what is now called The Nag Hammadi Scriptures, a collection of thirteen ancient books (called "codices") containing over fifty texts.

"They were discovered in Upper Egypt in 1945. This important discovery includes many primary "Gnostic Gospels" – texts once thought to have been destroyed during the early Christian struggle to define "orthodoxy" – scriptures such as the Gospel of Thomas, the Gospel of Philip, and the Gospel of Truth.

The discovery and translation of the Nag Hammadi library, initially completed in the 1970's, has provided impetus to a major re-evaluation of early Christian history..."[2]

In these scriptures, Jesus wasn't here to bring eternal salvation. He was here to teach that God and heaven are in each one of us and taught we should love one another. He didn't start a religion and never heard of Christianity. He was born, lived, and died a Jew.

The question then, is this being true, how did Jesus, one of many apocalyptic preachers of his time, influence the creation of one of the most influential philosophical forces in the world; a force that shaped Western civilization? He never wrote anything we know of; probably never traveled more than fifty miles from his birthplace, and only preached to Jews,

The answer is–he didn't. It was Paul, arguably the greatest salesman in the history of Western civilization.

Without Paul, Jesus' influence probably would have died with his brother James and those who stayed in Jerusalem after his crucifixion. Remember, those in Jerusalem were Jews and had no contact with Gentiles. Probably those disciples who left to evangelize would have had little effect on Gentiles. They were preaching to Jews in synagogues.

The historical truth is that Paul created Christianity as we know it. He was the one who preached to the Gentiles and financially supported those who remained in Jerusalem. And without the divinity story, even he may not have been very successful.

The key to Christian theology is the resurrection of Jesus, which supposedly proves his divinity. But the only event we can be historically certain of is his death at the hands of the Romans. His resurrection is a matter of faith and not evidence.

It's difficult to know exactly what transpired in the twenty-year period between Jesus' crucifixion and Paul's conversion experience on the road to Damascus. But one thing historians know for sure is the resurrection story spread as increasingly more Jews began to believe that Jesus was the messiah, the savior, and the son of God. And in doing so, began to form another sect within Judaism. But make no mistake; it was a Jewish sect, more precisely a Jesus-believing sect within Judaism. It was not Christianity as we know it today.

This sect was the very sect of Jews who Saul persecuted and condemned to imprisonment and death. Here, Saul's story gets interesting.

In traditional religious teachings, Saul's experience on the road to Damascus was an encounter with the spirit of the divine Jesus. It was the spirit of Jesus who asked him why he was persecuting him and his followers. During that few seconds, Saul's whole worldview changed, and he became the Paul we know today. He was completely transformed and became the 13th apostle appointed by God himself–as he claimed and tradition teaches.

Here's the question: Did Saul have a Near Death Experience, NDE, on the road to Damascus? Before you make up your mind, consider these facts.

NDE's[3] are Unexplained Consciousness Events that sometimes happen in periods when people are approaching death but do not die. UCE's also occur much more frequently during other times like deep meditation or prayer, periods of high stress or even in early childhood. They may have even happened to you when the phone rang, and you knew it was someone who you haven't heard from in years. You answered the phone, and it was that person calling. Or when you had a premonition that came true.

Speculating in this instance, Saul was under great stress, he was an intense, competitive man with big ambitions. Here, the last sentence in his letter to the Galatians give us a clue to his state of mind, "I was advancing in Judaism beyond many of my own age among my people and was extremely zealous for the traditions of my fathers."

Paul's stress was probably exacerbated when he thought of the scandal that a crucified, humble preacher from Galilee should be worshiped as the son of God. Keep in mind; the Romans crucified criminals to demonstrate contempt for them and left their dead bodies on the cross. A common practice done so wild animals could eat their remains to remind others of how lowly they were.

Think about how Paul felt knowing that this misguided heretical Jewish sect was promoting the idea that a crucified, humble preacher, a criminal, was the king of the Jews, the Messiah, the Son of God himself.

But the experience on the road was so powerful a revelation that it became the turning point in his life.

Acts 9 tells the story of Paul's conversion as a third-person narrative: "As he neared Damascus on his journey, suddenly a light from heaven flashed around him. He fell to the ground and heard a voice say to him, "Saul, Saul, why do you persecute me?"

"Who are you, Lord?" Saul asked.

"I am Jesus, whom you are persecuting," he replied. "Now get up and go into the city, and you will be told what you must do."

"The men traveling with Saul stood there speechless; they heard the sound but did not see anyone. Saul got up from the ground, but when he opened his eyes, he could see nothing. So, they led him by the hand into Damascus. For three days, he was blind and did not eat or drink anything. "— *Acts 9:3–9, NIV*

Different renditions don't agree regarding the specific events that occurred. For instance, whether his companions witnessed what Paul saw or not, this incident was the moment of his conversion. Another way of saying this is, like reports from other Near Death Experiencers, his whole life changed because of a single event that lasted only a few seconds.

There was the light, the voice, the recognition of the being, and the life review (acknowledgment of the pain he was causing other people in his life). All common elements in NDE's. But the most telling aspect of Paul's experience was the all-important, immediate life transformation that occurred as a result. In Paul's case, there were also the lasting psychosomatic effects of such a powerful experience; he was temporarily blinded. [4]

But it doesn't end here. Paul was converted to the very opposite of what he had spent his life trying to perfect; understanding and obeying the strictest laws of the Torah. In just a few seconds he went from that to offering his entire life to the belief that the single greatest commandment is to love. He believed that the traditional Jewish law that guided him his whole life did not need to be fulfilled. In this way, Paul's lesson was the same as that learned by other people who experience Near Death Experiences (NDEr's): "Consciously living by love is the essence of life itself."

So, this speculation based on the fundamental facts of Paul's conversion experience is that he had what we now call a near death experience. And if we were to deconstruct all the revisions, perversions, and re-interpretations of Christian theology, we might find the connection between what Paul taught and what NDEr's experience today. In thousands of authentic cases, every person learns the same lesson: learning to love is the most important learning objective in our lives.

As a side note: Later in this book, you will be introduced to the research of Oxford scholar, Dr. Gregory Shushan, showing compelling evidence for a startling proposal: NDE's are the basis of human belief in the afterlife and the core supernatural principles in religions.

As you contemplate this speculation about Christianity's origins, remember what I indicated above, Paul wrote before all the canonical gospels were written; at least two decades before Mark and as many as six decades before John. And as he emphasized throughout his authentic epistles [5] his revelation did not come from any other human being, but directly from the spirit of the dead Jesus. At least that's the way Paul described it. My question is simple: could that have been the loving voice in the light that all NDEr's experience?

Is it any wonder why Paul is considered by many to be the first Jewish-Christian mystic? Yes, his mysticism came from his experience on the road.

Our question is, did it come from an actual encounter with Jesus or was Paul reporting his experience in terms he could understand and communicate to others?

In other words, using the name of Jesus because that was the only way he could describe an experience, that like other NDEr's explain, is beyond human experience and consequently beyond common language to describe?

To repeat, if we were to trace the evolution of the numinous in the gospels, we would find that this idea advanced in each of the three synoptic gospels and finally culminated in John's gospel, the most esoteric of the four. Also, keep in mind that the reports from most NDEr's are expressed in culture-based language. The experiences are ineffable, beyond words. And thus, the experiencer tends to use language that most closely resembles their cultural or religious archetypes; in Paul's case, Jesus, whom he had intense feelings about during his efforts to persecute his followers.

Dusting off the interpretational sediments from two thousand years is an impossible challenge. We have a few original texts, but most of the oldest have been translated and re-interpreted dozens of times.

We're never going to know the exact truth about the whole Christian story. But despite the numerous horrors conducted in the name of Christianity, there remain certain core truths that resonate with us all these years later. They are the same truths taught in every NDE, usually described in cultural-religious language. Whoever the loving presence of the light may be, the message is always the same: Love is the essence of the universe.

If the focus on Christianity seems too limited, refer again to the research and work of Dr. Gregory Shushan, a research fellow at Oxford's Ian Ramsey Center for Science and Religion, and the author of the acclaimed Conceptions of the Afterlife in Early Civilizations.

During his presentation at the IANDS[6] conference in July of 2016, he asked a vital question. Did the concept of an afterlife come from religion or did it shape religion but come from NDE's? His research explores ancient civilizations for clues and finds them all the way back to 2350 BCE.

There is simply no question that the concept of an afterlife and the shaping of ancient religions are like the reports of NDE's. It is in the historical record for anyone to see. If you still have a question about the authenticity of NDE's as UCE's you can either purchase his book indicated above or watch his presentations on YouTube.

Decision Time

Here's the key question for you: At the very depths of your soul, does it make any difference if Paul had an authentic divinely inspired vision of Jesus or an encounter with a loving presence that all NDEr's have during authentic NDEs? The message is the same.

If it does make a difference and you need to adhere to your orthodoxy, this book may not be for you. But if you can live with the possibility of another way of getting the same message, you have the right book in your hands.

If you decide to proceed, get set for a crazy, exciting ride! The balance of this book will explore these Unexplained Consciousness Experiences from both a scientific perspective and a religious point of view.

After all these explanations and admonitions, if you've decided to buy the book, welcome to my world. It's full of wonders truly stranger than fiction.

Notes

Chapter 1

The Error of our ways

"If you don't know where you're going, any road will get you there."

Lewis Carroll

This world destroying itself because it has a wrong-headed notion of who we are: For instance, we think we are separate and distinct from each other and the space of the cosmos we occupy. In this Western view of the world, defending ourselves and those we love against the interest of others justifies, and some instances demands conflict.

This is key to human conflict in the West, and by extension, everywhere the West interferes. It is so subliminal that the average person is unaware of its power. It is the silent ontology that emerges from Newtonian Physics. (A reminder here is that ontology is our understanding of our existence.)

That's the materialistic, local, deterministic universe where everything that exists is described in separate and distinct concrete terms. In this world, actions and reactions are calculated by knowing initial and boundary conditions, the applicable entailing laws and doing the proper mathematical calculations. Consequently, every person is an individual with only his or her own interests to protect. And every problem has a single cause and cure. There is a right or wrong mutually exclusive solution to every conflict.

There's one major problem. It's killing us.

At the most basic level, the universe doesn't work this way. It is indeterminate and non-local, (holistic). Everything is linked to everything else. Everyone is connected to everyone else. Objects are spatial extensions, seemingly distinct but never separate from a primary coherent fabric from which everything comes: Very much like

19

a single ocean wave, a distinct form that appears as something apart for a time and returns to the body of water it never left. The universe is a complex system, and every part of a complex system affects every other part.

Some of the separatist symptoms of our Newtonian postmodern societal illnesses are reflected in our social constructions. We've created national borders, black, white, yellow, red, and brown people. We classify ourselves as Jews, Christians, Muslims, Hindus, Liberals, Moderates, Conservatives, Independents, and Libertarians. We decide who are winners and losers. We determine scarcity, abundance, labor, and capital. These are all artificial distinctions created by us.

In the West, these social constructions are based on the Newtonian understanding of reality with Einsteinian enhancements. Even the epistemological poles of empiricism and rationalism embodied and energized in the postmodern dialectic, arise from the distinctions created by Newton's mechanics.

So where do we go from here? If we recognize this is at the core of the complex conditions giving rise to the interminable and intractable human conflicts that plague us, what do we do now?

The surprise here is that Quantum Mechanics or QM has given us clues for at least a century. Both scientists and philosophers have known Newton's clockwork universe is only a partial explanation. And yet its influence remains the foundation of Western social constructions and our underlying ontology.

For change to happen, we must confront the particular ideologies that enshrine the Newtonian mechanical model of reality.

In this book, we will confront traditional science and revisionist postmodern religion. They've both become ideologies because, in their own ways, they're intractable despite any evidence to the contrary. And yes, although religion earns the most negative publicity today, it might surprise some that scientists are also prone to ideological defenses of favored theories and models. At the extremes, scientism, the belief that science alone will explain all phenomena, seems to have reached its limit.

One needs look no farther than the latest available findings at the Large Hadron Collider, LHC. They suggest that the sacred Standard

Model of Particle Physics, SMPP, may no longer accurately describe the subatomic level of our universe.

The problem is much broader than just our questions at the subatomic level. At the classical 3 D level that we experience, the shadow of the mechanistic model in Newton's mechanics permeates everything and this is understandable. Even Einstein, one of the most brilliant scientists in history, had lifelong difficulties accepting new findings in Quantum Mechanics. But as Max Planck[7] said, science like all other ideologies "makes progress one funeral at a time."

Our discovery of the quantum level of the universe shines a light on the dark space between epistemological poles of rationalism and empiricism. It has the potential to be the unifier between Newtonian discrete physicality and religious mysticism. It might even allow us to ground what we have called supernatural phenomenon in scientific models.

One thing is sure, what we call common-sense isn't sufficient to understand the universe. So what's the evidence for this claim?

Our common-sense fails us

For instance, here are a few examples:

- Our common sense tells us we experience solid objects in our reality. We now know what appears to have materiality or mass is at the most basic level pure energy.
- If we were to take all the space internal to, between and among the atoms that make up solid objects, there would remain minute amounts of seemingly material particles.
- For instance, if we could remove the space in all its atoms, the Empire State Building would fit into a teaspoon.
- These particles themselves are vibrating strings of energy.
- What we experience as a single cubic meter of "empty" interstellar space is filled with virtual quantum level particles constantly coming into and out of existence.
- That same cubic meter of empty space contains enormous amounts of energy, enough to boil all the oceans on earth.

Some call it the final free lunch of energy available to us when and if we figure out how to use it.

These are just a few examples of how our common sense fails us; none of which can be experienced directly by our normally functioning sensory systems.

What other wonders remain?

We can only explain about five percent of the universe. We know the balance is here because we can measure its effect on what we can explain. Not only do we not know what it is, we have inherent limitations in determining our questions. If our questions come from our current context, we risk limiting answers to that context.

If we legitimize these new discoveries and allow them to lead us where they will, we will find that the entire premise of a materialistic universe doesn't answer the essential human question: What is the full range of human possibilities?

So, we come to the fundamental paradox: Is this a purely materialistic universe, a cold, dark realm of indifference, in which life emerged by accident? Or is it a universe created by a petulant, sometimes vindictive creator so the souls of his human creations can be saved? But as I try to show in this book, the real universe is very different from either explanation.

Our knowledge of the quantum level has opened whole new areas of research and with it whole new horizons of discovery.

The only true barriers to changing this entire planet for the better are *unexamined* human presuppositions based on the fallacy of *separation* and *competition*. *Separation* intensified by propagandized fear for profit's sake. *Competition* intensified by a false belief in scarcity. These are all unexamined because we don't know what we don't know, but we think we know. And our religious and scientific ideologies prohibit further inverstigations unless they are consistent with existing models.

If we could reboot the whole system, it would help to remember that we designed it without conscious awareness of the end game. We are on an unsustainable trajectory of depletion, waste, and destruction of our only home.

Of course, there are powerful forces supported by vast fortunes holding these presuppositions in place. But as these fortunes grow and become more concentrated in the hands of the few, one can only hope the masses will wake up in time to save our species from the horrors of a dying planet and with that the end of life here. And we are well on way to this end point. Eight individuals own more wealth than 3.6 billion other people as of this writing.[8]

The life of the planet is not at stake. Once the damage of human consumption ends, the earth will cleanse itself and recover. We may not be here to enjoy it.

Notes

Chapter 2

The Urgency

"We live in a vacuous world, yet we do so with a feeling of urgency."

Astrid Berges-Frisbey

It's shameful that we're willing to tolerate the annihilation of other human beings. It's frightening that we're destroying the web of life that supports us as though we are somehow separate and distinct. For some reason, we think the pollution of the planet doesn't pollute our bodies and those of our loved ones. Why don't we realize that our perpetual wars and conflicts about our natural resources, our fear of scarcity in an environment of abundance, and our inability to see that the system doing the damage is of our own making?

We are so much more than our biology. Our planet is so much more than a rocky sphere of natural resources just waiting to be depleted by us. And at the core of this inability to recognize the damage we do is the mistaken notion that this universe is a mechanistic, indifferent, empty place with no meaning other that what we bring to it.

Evidence to the contrary has been in us and all around us for as long as we've been able to contemplate our existence. We've been aware of our possibilities from the earliest days of our conscious awareness.

For whatever the reasons, modernity has brought with it suspicions of the individual's subjective experience as a valid source of discovery and knowledge; unless that individual has the proper credentials. But in the last several decades, some people have been able to withstand the rejections that come from breaking the hypnotic trance of acceptance and take the risks necessary to open a new dialog that will eventually reveal the truth of our potential.

This time can be an inflection point, a change in direction in our downward spiral to complete destruction of our only home and we should pray that it is.

So just what is this incredible finding that promises such a change in direction? As one would expect it's not just what the finding is but what it represents. It represents a deeper understanding of human potential. It's not the popular, commercialized human potential associated with motivational programs or taught by positive-thinking gurus. It's the deeper awareness that comes from recognizing the link of human consciousness with the co-creation of the reality we perceive. It's the revelation that comes with a deeper understanding of the cosmos we inhabit. It's the full realization of what we can do as normal human beings and our role in the unfolding of the unique space of our individual experience. It's the power of human consciousness unveiled in what are being called Unexplained Consciousness Events or UCE's.

Unexplained Consciousness Events

I've used the phrase, *Unexplained Consciousness Events, UCEs,* to classify these kinds of experiences as falling out of the range of conventional explanations based on a Newtonian mechanistic model of reality. In other words, we cannot explain these consciousness events with our current scientific explanations of human consciousness. But there is something here that offers us an opportunity to ask new questions and in doing so, learn more about how we function in a universe that is vastly different from how we perceive it to be.

The reader's next question might be, "how does the universe being different from our perceptions make it worthy of investigation in this regard?"

There is a clue in this excerpt from an article by Amanda Gefter in Quanta Magazine, in September of 2016. She writes, "As we go about our daily lives, we tend to assume that our perceptions — sights, sounds, textures, tastes — are an accurate portrayal of the real world. Sure, when we stop and think about it — or when we find ourselves fooled by a perceptual illusion — we realize with a jolt that what we perceive is never the world directly, but rather our brain's best guess at what that world is like, a kind of internal simulation of an external reality. Still, we bank on the fact that our simulation is a reasonably decent one. If it wasn't, wouldn't evolution have eliminated us by now? The actual reality might be forever beyond our reach, but surely our senses give us at least an inkling of what it's really like."

Not so, says Donald D. Hoffman, a professor of cognitive science at the University of California, Irvine. Dr. Hoffman goes on to explain that "getting at questions about the nature of reality, and disentangling the observer from the observed, is an endeavor that straddles the boundaries of neuroscience and fundamental physics."

And with this statement he makes the great leap forward in developing an answer to the "hard problem" contained in the study of consciousness: "The hard problem of consciousness is the problem of explaining how and why we have qualia or phenomenal experiences— how sensations acquire characteristics, such as colors and tastes."

The philosopher David Chalmers, who introduced the term "hard problem" of consciousness, contrasts this with the "easy problems" of explaining the ability to discriminate, integrate information, report mental states, focus attention, etc. Easy problems are easy because all that is required for their solution is to specify a mechanism that can perform the function. That is, their proposed solutions, regardless of how complex or poorly understood they may be, can be entirely consistent with the modern materialistic conception of natural phenomena. Chalmers claims that the problem of experience is distinct from this set, and he argues that the problem of experience will "persist even when the performance of all the relevant functions is explained."

In effect, Chalmers is addressing the question of how can the brain obeying just the ordinary laws of physics as we currently understand them, create first-person conscious experience consisting of the internal representations of the things we see, hear, taste and touch. Another way of saying this is how can the brain, a physical object, create the mind, a non-physical phenomenon. And then how does the mind, a non-physical phenomenon, interact with the body, a physical object?

According to current science, this is psychokinesis[9] or PK, and that's considered pseudoscience.

Amid all the refutations and questionable explanations, there remains an open question: "How do we explain the phenomenon represented in the examples at the beginning of this book?

The merging of quantum physics with the cognitive and neurosciences promises to be a better road to answering this question.

Quantum Physics?

So, the next question is why? Why does the addition of quantum physics enhance the cognitive science investigator's toolkit? The answer lies in understanding the meta-structure upon which our whole body of scientific knowledge lies. More precisely, if we are going to revise our understanding of the universe, we must change that structure in such a way as to put consciousness at the foundation for all the rest. Currently, the meta-structure looks like this.

Consciousness
Psychology
Biology
Chemistry
Physics

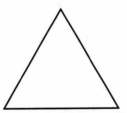

As you can see, our meta-structure of human knowledge is like a pyramid that starts with physics at the bottom. Then goes up to chemistry, leading up to biology. Then leads up to psychology, eventually reaching the hard problem of consciousness.

But all the experiments in quantum mechanics have repeatedly shown that consciousness is fundamental to the creation of the reality we perceive. Not just our personal experience as Dr. Hoffman describes above, but also the measurable outcomes of our scientific experiments. We first learned this with the double-slit experiment[10] and have proven it repeatedly for several decades. These findings suggest we should be putting consciousness at the foundation of our pyramid of knowledge.

Psychology
Biology
Chemistry
Physics
Consciousness

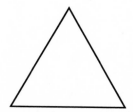

By placing consciousness at the foundation, we are saying our conscious observation creates our subjective experience, which is consistent with current cognitive science. We are also saying the scientific resistance to dualism is no longer a barrier to explaining consciousness. But the big leap is recognizing that together we co-create the universe within which we live. This shift opens the door to understanding Unexplained Consciousness Events as happening within the context of a monistic[11] scientific model and not as a feature of a mysterious supernatural realm.

Quantum physics has taught us contrary to the mechanistic model, the universe is not objective, separated, or deterministic. It is subjective, holistic, and non-deterministic. Our old mechanical model of a clockwork universe has been modified. At the most fundamental level of reality, it is a unified field of probability waves. To be precise, these waves represent the probability of particles that when observed or measured cause them to take a specific position given how we set up the experiment or observation. For instance, in the double slit experiment light can be a wave or a particle based on how it is observed.[12]

As this research has proven over and again, we cannot separate the observed from the observer. What this says in laymen's terms is we do not see, hear, feel, or touch a real world separate from us. The objects we sense are not separate physical things somehow hanging out there in the surrounding space. They are co-creations of our observations, connected, not separate from us, the individual conscious agents. And in the strictest interpretation, the observer *is* the observed. This awareness is not to say that there isn't an absolute objective reality, but that the portion we perceive is a product of our interactions with it.

It's Not Turtles

It's individual conscious agents all the way down. In fact, the world we experience is a collection of the observations of multiple individual conscious agents including every sentient life form, not just human beings. A kind of matrix of consciousness creating what appears as our objective reality that doesn't exist as we think it does. It's difficult to understand, I know. An example might help.

This again from the same article by Amanda Gefter, Dr. Hoffman explains, "There's a metaphor that's only been available to us in the past 30 or 40 years, and that's the desktop interface. Suppose there's a blue rectangular icon on the lower right corner of your computer's desktop—does that mean the file itself is blue and rectangular and lives in the lower right corner of your computer? Of course, not. But those are the only things that can be asserted about anything on the desktop—it has color, position, and shape. Those are the only categories available to you, and yet none of them are true about the file itself or anything in the computer. They couldn't possibly be true. That's an interesting thing. You could not form a true description of the innards of the computer if your entire view of reality was confined to the desktop. And yet the desktop is useful. That blue rectangular icon guides my behavior, and it hides a complex reality that I don't need to know. That's the key idea. Evolution has shaped us with perceptions that allow us to survive. They guide adaptive behaviors. But part of that involves hiding from us the stuff we don't need to know. And that's pretty much all of reality, whatever reality might be".

So, as we cannot envision the actual "innards" or the insides of our computers by seeing the user interface, we cannot envision the actual "innards" of the reality we're so fond of arguing about.

Taking this metaphor a bit further, each of us is the computer operator. Our sensory systems are the graphic user interface, the system that interacts with the internal and external data. They are our computer screens. By our directions, our sensory systems call up the arrangements of particles that make up what we observe in our subjective experience. (on the computer screens of our lives)

Think of it this way; the underlying reality is like the contents of a computer file on our screen. It appears there in a form that we can comprehend. It doesn't remotely resemble what it looks like in the memory of our computers. Our request to observe it makes it a recognizable computer file. We are not seeing the actual nature of the electrons that make it up any more than we see the actual reality of our universe.

New Philosophical Challenges

These findings bring about serious concerns for philosophers. The most general area of philosophy, ontology, "the philosophical study of the nature of being, becoming, existence or reality"[13] examines the question of our basic nature. In other words, what is the true nature of our existence? And for that question to be answered, we must re-examine another philosophical area of study, epistemology. Because epistemology studies the validity of the information we seek to answer the ontological question.

So, the key question then is how do we know what we know about the nature of our existence?

Until about a century ago, we explained the universe as a gigantic mechanical machine, a clockwork universe, based on Newton's principles with Einsteinian enhancements. With the discovery of the quantum level, we know this model is incomplete. It's incomplete because we found that actions don't obey Newton's laws at the subatomic or quantum level of the universe. It appears the universe obeys two different sets of laws at two different levels. Newton's laws at the Classical level, the 3D level we experience, and quantum laws at the subatomic level that we cannot directly experience.

Therefore, philosophically we are left with an incomplete explanation of the nature of existence, our ontology, and questions about what constitutes valid knowledge, our epistemology, about that very question.

The discovery of quantum mechanics has changed the scientific model. Much like Copernicus changed the entire meta-structure of knowledge from the Earth at the center of the universe to the sun being the center of our solar system. This paradigm shift opened the door to a new cosmology[14] and with it a new understanding of the nature of our existence, (our ontology). This allowed us to ask new questions; new questions that could not have been asked in the old model. These new questions created the need to question the source of our knowledge. It create a new for a new epistemology.

Although this book is a plunge into a new way of thinking about who we are and how the universe works, the questions provoked by quantum physics are much too big for general answers in a layman's book. Consequently, I've tried to translate a great deal of complex material into rather simple explanations without the math.

No math was harmed while writing this book

Full disclosure: The math involved goes beyond my capability to understand, let alone use as an explanatory platform. (Even so, I crashed and bashed my way through enough of it to comprehend the basic theories so I could make them accessible to the innumerate among us – like me. I hope I succeeded.)

Without the math, it seemed important to pick something very human that we could all understand yet would provoke curiosity and maintain interest. Unexplained Consciousness Events, UCE's seemed to fit the bill. They allow us to concentrate our exploration; a practical example of how we and this universe might be working very differently from our previous ways of understanding. So, the choice is UCE's.

As you can readily see, the six examples used at the beginning are different in nature. Each offers an interesting opportunity to research, and each would result in volumes of new findings. But the purpose in this book is to examine only one form of UCE. And, it is the prime example of all UCE's, the Near Death Experience or NDE.

UCE's as NDE's

If we were having a casual conversation and I tried to convince you that there is something unexplainably authentic happening when another human being reports having a Near Death Experience, (NDE) you might have a good chuckle and think me daft. I know, because that's exactly what I did think when I read some reports. And of course, there's no shortage of scientists and skeptics who've made careers of debunking even the most credible reports. But there remain some that are convincing.

Let's look at the issue from another perspective. Many of these reports belong in the trash heap with other magical thinking and religious mythologies. But there are some, as we will see, that bear some deeper examination. Unfortunately, even these run the risk of being classified and labeled as sensationalized grandstanding and dismissed out of hand. Then it's a short distance to ignoring them as the natural physiological effects of the dying brain or superstitious claptrap.

In fact, there are undeniably valid reports about NDE's as Unexplained Consciousness Events that defy our common sense. These are the UCE's that provide clues to a need for a different understanding of how we and the universe function. This need is driven by the fact that many of these events defy any rational, scientific, or medical way of explaining them.

Important Caution

There's an important caution here. This book runs the risk of being disregarded because it includes the terms *Quantum Mechanics* and *Near Death Experiences*. There are probably no phrases being misused more to conjure up crazy ideas and convince the vulnerable public to buy useless products and services than Quantum Physics and Near Death Experiences.

In this book, we examine one form of UCE, the NDE. It is one way of exploring the mysteries revealed in quantum mechanics without the complex math. In doing so, we're not supporting or denying the results of other areas of investigation like Psi[15] or paranormal phenomenon. There are no assertions either for or against religious faith. And certainly no attempt to create fantasies about mystical properties that defy the laws of nature.

The arguments use legitimate science and grounded philosophy as foundations. The conclusions reached are not offered as doctrinal truths. And the word speculation is used frequently because, as written at the beginning, this book should properly be classified as speculative non-fiction.

Not being a scientist or professional philosopher doesn't equate to not having an insatiable curiosity about what it means to be a human being and the range of our possibilities. Most of us possess the curiosity and some the persistence to want answers to questions that seem to fit the experience of almost every person we know.

To go directly to the core question, we, and specifically that portion we call our brains, are probably the most complex organism in the known universe. How could we not want to know as much as we can about the full range of our possibilities?

This is certain, we don't yet understand all the laws of nature fully. We do have a natural tendency to throw out new discoveries if they don't fit the old models or meta-structures of knowledge. The main fear is that we will disregard the clues and signals coming to us from UCE's and miss an important tool in understanding our possibilities.

All those disclaimers offered, we use what are titled NDE's as a type of UCE for two important reasons. 1) Many of these near death reports sound exactly like scientific descriptions of the fundamental nature of the universe that seem beyond the normal ranges of our sensory systems. That is, descriptions coming to us from well-known and respected theoretical physicists. 2) These consciousness events happen when, per our current understanding of consciousness, all the subject's *consciousness equipment* [16] is turned off.

Consequently, NDE's provide a precise focus point, a well-defined search area to examine one type of UCE and how differences between the Newtonian and Quantum models[17] of physical reality might help us understand what they are all about.

As we saw in the beginning, there are many kinds of UCE's and trying to classify and show the differences in theoretical terms becomes an onerous task. It's certainly larger than can be covered in one book. But by using a practical example, an NDE, it seems a better way to approach a complex topic. Also, there is a vast body of NDE research literature to use as a resource.

One might ask why examine any of these events at all? The answer is simple. For all written human history, people from every corner of the world have made the same observation, "there's something more than our physical experience." The answers never quite satisfy us. "It's a religious experience," or "it's just your imagination," or "you need to be medicated."

We will learn more by illuminating the dark space that results from our inability or unwillingness to probe what lies beyond our theoretical models. It seems to be easier to accept incomplete answers and be done with it. The problem is that we begin to believe those incomplete answers and then insist that our worldview is correct. When we do, our worldview becomes an ideology, and our resistance is complete. If the current condition of the world isn't reason enough to find another way, what would be?

Resistance to New Learning

So why do we have such a difficult time opening to new learning? This difficulty can be explained as something called *certainty*. And *certainty* is justified by one's epistemology. In other words, the source and basis of the knowledge we consider valid. When our epistemologies differ, there is very little room for dialogue. There's very little room to explore and discover. One doesn't need to look any further than the political polarity in the world today. It is a battle of epistemologies.

In this case, even with all of this study and information about near death experiences, some readers will still resist accepting what they read. Consequently, this book consists of two major sections: The first section presents studies, reports, and speculations about Near Death Experiences (NDE's) as UCE's, including how emerging findings in cognitive science and theoretical physics might offer insights to understand this phenomenon better. For those readers who can accept them as something authentic and meaningful that merits further thought, this will suffice and section two is optional reading– interesting but optional.

The second section is for those readers who read the reports of NDE's and want to understand their resistance to accepting them. They see them as authentic and meaningful UCE's that merit further study. It's titled, "True or False."

In summary, so much of what troubles us today is our commitment to a tangled web of what we hold as *doctrinal truths* that conflict with each other. In other words, if you're paying attention, it's a confusing time to be alive. So, while this book tries to dislodge the reader from his or her vice-like grip on "doctrinal truths", it would be intellectually dishonest to offer replacements. There are no concrete certainties in this book. There are just questions and more than a few speculations. Remember, this book is speculative non-fiction, and hopefully will start new conversations for possibilities. There are no absolute answers here.

Notes

Chapter 3

The Closed Loop: Ontology – Epistemology - Ontology

"When faith collides with experiments, disagreements invariably arise. We usually think of this conflict in terms of religion vs. science. But sometimes disagreements arise because scientific faith clashes with repeated human experiences."

Dean Radin

Scientific faith can become an ideology based on what we refer to as an Einsteinian Epistemology[18]. There is then a hidden ontology[19] that emerges and becomes an obstacle to further investigation of that which does not fit this scientific model. For instance, "ontologically we are biological bags of cells, and by identifying each of our component subsystems, we will completely explain life. Epistemologically, science will give us the answers that justify and support that belief."

This is the closed loop, "ontology – epistemology – ontology" by which we interpret, re-interpret, and run the risk of misinterpreting our recurring human experiences.

By now it's obvious, to appreciate the arguments in this book, readers should be familiar with the terms ontology and epistemology. In fact, for readers to understand their reluctance to examine what may seem counter-intuitive, they should become familiar with these terms.

The reason is simple: these two terms identify the foundation upon which we build the social constructions that form our points of views.

This is not an easy task. Even as I research the literature to write this book, I hold a certain deep resistance to accepting what I find.

A reminder: Ontology is our mostly subconscious understanding of the nature of existence. Epistemology is the source of the knowledge we consider valid to support that subconscious understanding of the nature of our existence. These are both mostly buried deep in our subconscious presuppositions about the world. Another example might help to clarify.

39

Ontologically, some of us believe we exist as body and soul. This belief is called dualism. If we do, we depend on a source of information and knowledge usually traced back to Western religion. In simple terms, Christian traditions tell us that this is so. In this case, our epistemological bases are Christian texts, narratives, and traditions. We go to them to validate our points of views.

On the other hand, there are some who believe we are simply body and there is no soul or supernatural level of the universe. This belief is called monism. In simple terms, these people don't consider Christian texts to be a valid source of knowledge and information, at least as is necessary to inform their ontological beliefs, i.e., the nature of our existence. They go to scientific sources for their answers.

The conflict between dualism and monism becomes more complicated when we address new scientific findings. Einsteinian Epistemology becomes an obstacle. It contains the remnants of the Newtonian understanding of the universe which includes an objective reality based on a mechanistic and determinist clockwork view of the universe. That is, what is called a local universe where objects are disconnected and separated by space, and actions and reactions are predicted given known local conditions. This model is called classical physics and "classical physics rests upon five basic assumptions regarding the fabric of reality: an objective reality, locality, causality, continuity, and determinism." (Radin, 2009)

Now we know these assumptions don't provide an accurate picture of the quantum, or fundamental, level of the universe. Ontologically, classical physics no longer fully describes the nature of reality. Our bias is to look at every discovery through the lenses of the Einsteinian Epistemological model.

A practical example of the clash between ontologies and epistemologies is the ongoing war between secularism and fundamentalism in the world today. Science and Secularism are based on an ontology of materialism that suggests only physical reality exists. Therefore, there is no afterlife to worry us so we should go for it today. Enjoy the material things in life and have as much fun as you can. Its epistemology is mostly non-religious and usually materialistically and scientifically based. It doesn't consider religious texts to be particularly useful in providing valid knowledge about the nature of reality.

On the other hand, ontologically we have religious people who believe there is a supernatural level of reality. They believe they have a soul and a better life awaits their souls if they live guided by certain principles based on transcendent truths. Epistemologically, they find the knowledge they consider valid in their religious texts.

If these examples still seem remote, you can examine the current political scene to understand the power of ontology and epistemology to define how we see the world. Argue an opposite point of view against someone from the other side of the political polarity and listen for their beliefs about people (ontology). And listen for where they get the information they consider valid. (epistemology) It's almost guaranteed that although your end goals might be the same, you will see the same issues differently.

Or here's another example, the conflict between a creationist and an evolutionist can never be resolved as long as each looked to their respective sources of knowledge exclusively. The creationist might look to the Bible for guidance. The evolutionist might look to Darwin for guidance. The argument would remain unresolved because they value different sources of information.

My key point here is the important differences and obstacles to new discoveries are what we already believe about our basic nature and what kind of information we consider valid to inform and justify those beliefs. New information must be screened through a background narrative of "already knowing." And from here it's too easy to dismiss new discoveries.

We could identify another several dozen or so limitations in human cognition, but they would take us far afield from our topic. Suffice to say that we know very little with certainty and an open mind is a wonderful thing to have, even though it is one of the most difficult challenges in human experience.

A Major Challenge to Our Philosophical and Scientific Belief Systems

The key reason to focus on the issues of *ontology*[20] and *epistemology*[21] is they are the primary obstacles to change we all face when trying to absorb new information: The information that has the potential to shift our view of ourselves and the universe within which we live. The information needed to become new observers of the same reality. Consequently, they are the primary levers of change focused on throughout this book.

With Near Death Experiences, NDE's, we have the opportunity of a new area of inquiry about the nature of consciousness and with it a new explanation of what it means to be a sentient being in a vastly different universe than we ever suspected it to be. As this inquiry continues, it can change the conversation at both poles of the debate, religious and scientific.

Important Caveat

It is important to note that we should approach the phenomenon of NDE's with a good deal of caution. To be precise, we are interested in them as examples of unexplained consciousness events only if they have some veridical data we cannot explain in our usual ways. For instance, (1) there are many instances when an NDE'r could sense something they could not have known because of the proximity of the events they reported. Or they were blocked from hearing or seeing activities or objects in the room where they reported an NDE that was later proved to be accurate. (2) When an NDE'r had that consciousness experience with veridical criteria but had flat line EEG's.[22]

Although volumes of data from investigations of NDE's show a common structure of experiences including other phenomenon, we've chosen to concentrate on those that simply defy common sense explanations and are validated by other people. These examples are as close as we can get to intersubjective verification of a personal experience.

As an illustration of my point, here the author confronts one of the most respected theories in the medical and cognitive sciences. Consider that the theories he refers to are based on the empirical epistemology of science and inform an ontology that implies we are simply biological beings whose highest capacity, consciousness, is a secondary function of our brains. Which is wrongly considered, as is the rest of our physical body, a separate object from the universe?

"Despite differences of detail and interpretation, all of these theories have in common that the essential substrate for conscious experience – the neuroelectric activities that make it possible and that constitute or directly reflect the necessary and sufficient conditions for its occurrence – consist of synchronous or at least coherent high-frequency (gamma band, roughly 30 – 70 Hz) EEG oscillations linking widely separated, computationally specialized, regions of the brain.

"An enormous amount of empirical evidence supports these mind-brain correlations under normal conditions of mental life, and we do not dispute this evidence. The conventional interpretation of this correlation, however – that the observed neuroelectric activity itself generates or constitutes the conscious experience – must be incorrect, because, in both general anesthesia and cardiac arrest, the specific neuroelectric conditions that are held to be necessary and sufficient for conscious experience are abolished – and yet vivid, even heightened, awareness, thinking, and memory formation can still occur." (Irreducible Mind, Toward a Psychology for the 21st Century, 2007)

Obviously, something else is at work here, not explainable with knowledge within the boundaries of the ideologically empirical or the fervently religious epistemological poles. Even so, I offer what follows with a healthy dose of skepticism. These are not assertions. They may not even be valid assessments, but rather speculations. So, you'll find no new answers in what follows. Just more questions that naturally derive from seeing the same events as though through new eyes.

But Wait, There's More

Given the above qualifications I offered for using a specific type of NDEr's reports as a focal point for understanding UCE's, there was a more urgent reason for even considering them at all. The following quotes caused me to question how I was thinking about NDE's and take a closer look. How could a layperson with no scientific education, having an NDE describe the fundamental nature of reality as accurately as a trained theoretical physicist?

To be specific, a Near Death Experiencer reports, "Simultaneously, the time and the space on the other side was completely alive, evidential and real. Yes, while I was in the light, I had…[no] sense of the serial nature of time…past, present and future. All times, (the past, present and future) were experienced at every moment in time while I was in the light".

Brian Greene, theoretical physicist, writes, "If that reality encompasses all the events in spacetime, the total loaf exists. Just as we envision all of space really being out there, as really existing, we should also envision all of time as really being out there, as really existing too. The only thing that's real is the whole picture of spacetime".

So, as the reader can see in the above two quotes, the description reported by a person after a Near Death Experiences (NDE's) sounded exactly like the very explanations given by some of the most respected theoretical physicists and philosophers of our time. Not only Brian Greene but people like Marcelo Gleiser, Steven Hawking, Stuart Kauffman, Freeman Dyson, David Chalmers, Bernard d'Espagnat, Max Planck, Richard Feynman and Roger Penrose.

So just what is a near death experience or NDE?

From a paper by Dr. David San Filippo, National-Louis University, "According to a 1991 Gallup Poll estimate, 13 million Americans, 5% of the population, reported they have had a near-death experience (Greyson, 1992). Research has demonstrated that near-death experiences are no more likely to affect the devoutly religious than the agnostic or atheist. Near-death experiences can be experienced by anyone (Moody, 1975, 1977, 1980, Morse, 1990; Ring, 1980, 1985). According to Talbot (1991), near-death experiences appear to have no relationship to "a person's age, sex, marital status, race, religion and/or spiritual beliefs, social class, educational level, income, frequency of church attendance, size of home community, or area of residence.

"At the onset of the near-death experience, the individual may experience a sense of being dead, and surprise at being dead, yet will remain peaceful and have no feelings of pain. Following the peaceful awareness of being dead, the experiencer may have an out-of-body experience, a perception of separating from the physical body and moving away from the deceased body.

"The individual may experience a sense of moving through a tunnel, during the stage of entering into the darkness. As the individual passes through the tunnel, there may be an awareness of a bright light towards the end of the tunnel.

"While experiencing the consciousness of the light, ethereal forms recognizable by the experiencer may be seen in the light. In the later part of the near-death experience, the individual may sense he or she is rising rapidly towards the light into what he or she may consider heaven or another plane of consciousness.

"During this ascension, the experiencer may encounter a Being of Light reported to be either God, another spiritual deity, or an energy form recognized by non-theists. The encounter with the Being of Light engulfs the experiencer with a sense of unconditional love emanating from the Being.

"During this encounter, the near-death experiencer may become conscious of having a total panoramic review of his or her life and may experience a sense of self-judgment when observing his or her life events in review. The judgment is not by the Being of Light but is a personal judgment by the experiencer.

"Throughout each of the stages, and particularly in the latter stages of the near-death experience, the individual may be reluctant to return to his or her former life.

"Although most near-death reports are positive, in that they are pleasurable experiences, there are some reports of negative or "hellish" type experiences. The reports of negative near-death experiences appear to be rare. Of all the reported near-death experiences, a 1982 Gallup poll estimated that less than 1% are considered to be negative, hellish, and frightening experiences.

"The negative near-death experiences are reported to contain similar traits as positive experiences but are associated with a sense of extreme fear, panic or anger, a sense of helplessness, and possible visions of demonic creatures."

The professionally validated reports of Near Death Experiences, NDE's,[23] seem to offer subjective verification of current scientific theories of the fundamental nature of the universe.

In summary, lay people, with no formal scientific or medical training are providing descriptions that validate complex scientific theories.

A significant portion of NDEr's have consciousness experiences, seeing actions and hearing conversations, that are later verified by other people, many of them medical professionals. And they happen when their eyes are taped shut, with clicking devices in their ears and no sign of brain activity.

These facts beg the question. How?

Notes

Chapter 4

The Study of Near Death Experiences

"The world is not to be narrowed till it will fit into the understanding.... but the understanding to be expanded and opened till it can take in the image of the world as it is."

Francis Bacon

The Near Death Experience (NDE) is one of the most controversial topics one can examine. Today there are so many serious professionals investigating them, it's difficult to find a place to take a position. Are they real or are they a hoax played on a gullible public? A public that yearns to know what happens after death. Because of this human yearning, the field is filled with charlatans.

But there is a reason to believe some portion of NDE reports is authentic. These are difficult to dismiss. The problem is that the search area is too broad to allow impartial reporting of those events that call for a serious investigation. This problem allows so many misguided interpretations, the field runs the risk of being completely dismissed as without value in the study of consciousness.

But something has happened in the last hundred years that provides a new lens through which to view the fundamental functions of the cosmos that for decades has been described with the deterministic laws of Newton's clockwork universe. Now we're are developing a new understanding of the basic nature of the universe and with it a new perspective on human consciousness. Maybe now we can explore NDE's more fully.

Philosophers and physicists know the reason is the discovery of the quantum level of the universe. The sub-atomic foundation of reality that is several levels of abstraction removed from our experience here at the classical level.

The quantum level and every level below is radically different from how we have understood reality. These non-intuitive discoveries have caused us to re-think so much of what we have previously believed. Today we are seeing those early religious teachings were attempts to provide us with a language to describe what humankind has always sensed is here and couldn't figure out scientifically. (As written very early in this book, Dr. Gregory Shushan, has researched and found evidence of the effects of NDE's on ancient religions as far back as 2350.) (Shushan, 2011)

At the risk of sounding poetic, we might say our search for God is the same as our search for the origin of everything. In Eastern tradition, it is the infinite silence that is the basis of the universe and universal consciousness.

It is important to recognize that this revised meta-structure eliminates the scientific objection to the need for dualism. That is, the objection to any explanation of non-matter interacting with physical matter. It places consciousness and physical matter in the same plane of existence, the material universe, thereby removing the objection to dualism.

It's also consistent with what we find when our consciousness interacts with the physical objects in our scientific experiments. What we're seeing is the functioning of a non-local, connected universe that doesn't require an external mechanism to communicate with itself instantly.

Probably the most powerful awareness to come from this new way of understanding the universe is that it includes us. As sentient beings of this universe, we consist of the same "stuff" as all its levels. We appear as individuals emerging as such when conditions are met to create us. In Buddhist terms, this is like what is called dependent origination.[24]

We are not distinct objects hanging in midair apart from our surroundings. We are not distinct at all. There are no isolated systems in the universe. As Einstein said, "Physical objects are not in space, but these objects are spatially extended as fields."

Think of a spatial extension as a wave on the surface of the ocean. We are in constant unity with the underlying structure of the universe as the wave is with the ocean. But because of our subjective experience and egos we think of ourselves as separate and apart.

Our deepest meditations and prayers are a search for the experience of the infinite silence, or if you prefer, God, at the basis of reality, like the depths of the ocean of consciousness that exists within us. This is the unlimited consciousness we are born into. In Eastern thinking, this is the clear light of consciousness that we return to at biological death.

This most recent era of discovery has launched new studies of consciousness and how our brains function. For instance, Dr. Stuart Hameroff, M.D. Anesthesiologist, is convinced consciousness is not just "turned off" but disconnected when we are under an anesthetic. Consistent with the above meta-structure, he speculates that the origin of consciousness is somewhere other than the brain which opens the door to a different understanding of UCE's.

He goes on to propose how our brains are quantum-sensitive organs and how consciousness is an interaction with the quantum. But it needn't stop with our brains. If you think about the fact that our presence at the 3 D classical level of the universe emerges from the quantum level, consciousness permeates our entire body. To be clear, if consciousness is universal and fundamental to all reality, it exists in everything, including every cell in our body.

What's astounding to me is that Eastern thinking has held to this ontology of wholeness and connectivity for thousands of years.

A speculation: Our brains may simply be the primary area of our body that has evolved to allow us to be cognizant of a universal consciousness at this level of reality.

As an example, neuroscientists tell us that our brains work to organize our sensory input so that even the involvement of time itself is modified to make our subjective experience seem coordinated, whole and complete.

Our sensory systems function at different speeds and without our brains' modification, nothing would seem co-ordinated. For instance, the visual experience of clapping hands would not match the sound of them, if our brains didn't "stitch" the whole experience together. The key point here is our internal experience of external reality is moderated by our brains, so we have a holistic interpretation of life around us. A gestalt, so to speak; an organized whole, perceived as more than the sum of its parts.

As we have seen, we are evolutionarily adapted to fit this level of reality but not perceive the actual universe as it functions.

Dr. Stuart Kauffman M.D., theoretical biologist, and complex systems researcher has even shown evidence of how the brain functions at the quantum level in microtubules in the cells in our brains. In other words, this may be the way our brain assists in the creation of 3D consciousness but is not the sole source of all the consciousness awareness we are capable of, as evidenced in UCE's.

Recent discoveries have shown that certain birds are using quantum calculations to aid in their migrations. We know the process of photosynthesis depends on quantum actions. We even know that smell, once thought to be a purely chemical process, is a process of hearing because the molecules we think we smell are interacting at the quantum level and are converted to vibrations that we hear.

Taking this information a bit deeper and broader, the universe seems to be a large field of vibrations of varying frequencies that we perceive as energy and matter. As Nikola Tesla proposed, "think of the universe in terms of energy, frequency, vibration."

According to the latest model of particle physics, what we perceive as physical matter is resistance. It comes from the difference in frequencies as subatomic particles resist each other. (Think of the how magnets repel each other as though there is something material between them.)

To make the questions even more interesting, putting consciousness at the base of the universe, opens the door to the question, does it contain information about the experiences of every sentient creature, an idea familiar in Eastern thinking? Some say yes and think that people in more sensitive states and children under five have greater access to this universal information.

This belief might explain memories of previous lives in regression and children knowing details of other lives usually explained by reincarnation. It also might explain child-prodigies who demonstrate skill mastery and knowledge beyond their years at very early ages.

This sensitivity could also be true during dreams, meditation, and hypnosis. It's also possible that some select individuals are born with this increased sensitivity. This idea would go a long way to explaining UCE's. Think about how this may explain the UCE's that I mentioned in the introduction to this book.

It also might explain findings by Dr. Jim Tucker, M.D., at the Division of Perceptual Studies, University of Virginia. He has amassed over 2500 validated cases of reincarnation. Is it a coincidence that he has found that most people who remember past lives do so before they are five or six years old. After that age, the memories fade and disappear?

So, some of these examples are just theories, and some are proven scientific facts. I offer them to jolt our minds into thinking outside the usual box of Newtonian physics.

Take a moment and consider how you are reacting to reading this information. Is it difficult to grasp? Or is it difficult to allow that there is something here that lies outside of your common sense ways of understanding–your previous way of thinking about reality? Yes, that reality. The one we subjectively co-create and call objective.

Much investigation remains to be done before we can determine the validity of some scientific theories, while others are factual examples of new discoveries in science. None the less, it's important to note that the critical connection here is a new way of understanding the universe that came with the discovery of the quantum level and ongoing discoveries in the cognitive sciences. Together, they are creating a different model of reality. A model that allows us to re-think those theories that limit our understanding of how our consciousness works and how we function in the universe. A model that allows us to reimagine a world of connectedness with fewer conflicts and less violence.

We live in a very different kind of universe than we ever thought could exist. A universe that is not a fixed, deterministic, mechanical place but one where we participate in its creation. It's a cosmos where the illusion of solid matter is resistance to oscillations with different frequencies. It's a place where consciousness plays a key role in its existence, and where our explanations of our reality are impoverished at best and completely obsolete at the worst.

This model allows us to investigate UCE's with the hope of a more grounded understanding.

For the following, be aware of your natural position of "already knowing" and read this list of examples that might seem counterintuitive. This list is just a sampling of a few findings on the site, *near-death.com*, that shows the level of investigation and in some instances even make compelling arguments for the authenticity of reports from NDEr's:

- Cardiologist Michael Sabom described a near-death experience that occurred while its experiencer - a woman who was having an unusual surgical procedure for the safe excision and repair of a large basilar artery aneurysm - met all of the accepted criteria for brain death. (She was able to describe events in the operating room she had no way of knowing about,)

- Dr. Bruce Greyson documented perhaps one of the most compelling examples of a person who had an NDE and observed events while outside of his body which were later verified by others. The only way that these events could have been observed by the experiencer was if, in fact, he was outside of his body.

- Dr. Kenneth Ring and Sharon Cooper completed a two-year study into the NDEs of the blind. They published their findings in a book entitled "Mindsight" in which they documented the solid evidence of 31 cases in which blind people report visually accurate information obtained during an NDE.

- On Oct. 23, 2000, The BBC reported: "Evidence of Life After Death" about a study in the UK conducted by Dr. Sam Parnia and others at the University of Southampton which provided scientific evidence suggesting the survival of consciousness after clinical and brain death.

- Pim van Lommel led a study concerning the NDEs of research subjects who had a cardiac arrest. The findings of the study suggest that research subjects can experience consciousness, with self-identity, cognitive function, and memories, including the possibility of perception outside their body (autoscopy), during a flat EEG. Those research subjects who had NDEs report that their NDE was a bonafide preview of the afterlife.

- One particular theory of consciousness which is supported by NDE research involves the concept of consciousness expansion after death. Stanislav Grof, a leading consciousness researcher, explained this theory in the documentary entitled "Life After Death" by Tom Harpur: "My first idea was that it [consciousness] has to be hard-wired in the brain. I spent quite a bit of time trying to figure out how something like that is possible. Today, I came to the conclusion that it is not coming from the brain. In that sense, it supports what Aldous Huxley believed after he had some powerful psychedelic experiences and was trying to link them to the brain. He came to the conclusion that maybe the brain acts as a kind of reducing valve that protects us from too much cosmic input ... I don't think you can locate the source of consciousness. I am quite sure it is not in the brain – not inside of the skull ... It actually, according to my experience, would lie beyond time and space, so it is not localizable.

- Dr. Melvin Morse was an Associate Professor of Pediatrics at the University of Washington. He has studied near-death experiences in children for over 15 years and is the author of several outstanding books on the subject.

- Perhaps the best example of a person having an NDE and bringing back a scientific discovery from it is the NDE of Lynnclaire Dennis (www.mereon.org). Another example of bringing back scientific discoveries resulting from an NDE comes from Mellen-Thomas Benedict. After his NDE, Mellen-Thomas Benedict brought back a great deal of scientific information   concerning biophotonics, cellular communication, quantum biology, and DNA research. Mellen-Thomas Benedict currently holds eight U.S. patents and is always working on more.

- In a hospital in Switzerland in 1944, the world-renowned psychiatrist Carl G. Jung had a heart attack and then a near-death experience. His vivid encounter with the light, plus the intensely meaningful insights led Jung to conclude that his experience came from something real and eternal.

- New developments in quantum physics show that we cannot know phenomena apart from the observer. Arlice Davenport challenges the hallucination theory of NDEs as outmoded because the field theories of physics now suggest new paradigm options available to explain NDEs. Mark Woodhouse argues that the traditional materialism/dualism battle over NDEs may be solved by Einstein.

- In 1977, Dr. Kenneth Ring was a brilliant young professor of psychology at the University of Connecticut who read Dr. Raymond Moody's book, Life After Life and was inspired by it. However, he felt that a more scientifically structured study would strengthen Moody's findings. He sought out 102 near-death survivors for his research. He concluded: "Regardless of their prior attitudes - whether skeptical or deeply religious - and regardless of the many variations in religious beliefs and degrees of skepticism from tolerant disbelief to outspoken atheism - most of these people were convinced that they had been in the presence of some supreme and loving power and had a glimpse of a life yet to come."

- Dr. Jeffrey Long is a physician practicing the specialty of radiation oncology in Houma, Louisiana. Dr. Long served on the Board of Directors of IANDS and is actively involved in NDE research. In his book, "Evidence of the Afterlife: The Science of Near-Death Experiences," Dr. Long documents a study he conducted the largest scientific study of NDEs ever. It is based on his research of over 1,300 NDEs shared with NDERF.org.

- Researchers at the Coma Science Group, directed by Steven Laureys, and the University of Liege's Cognitive Psychology Research, headed by Professor Serge Bredart and Hedwige Dehon, have demonstrated that the physiological mechanisms triggered during NDEs lead to a more vivid perception not only of imagined events in the history of an individual but also of real events which have taken place in their lives."

Skepticism

It becomes obvious to those who are interested in seriously examining NDE's on a broader basis there exists a major split in similar reports. Like the above, some are authentic. And admittedly, this list is what remains of an even greater list of debunked reports that don't belong in serious scientific investigations. Like all popular phenomenon, there are as many detractors as there are serious investigators. And those serious skeptics help to clean up the data.

None the less, the nature of skepticism is very personal. We become aware of something that doesn't fit our worldview, and we are skeptical. Very often, we simply reject out of hand most of what doesn't fit. In the process of rejecting information, subconsciously we are accepting our sources of our knowledge without question.

But what happens when we question our own epistemology? In other words, that source or sources we consider to be the valid information? This questioning is not an easy process. Because when we question the source of the information we consider valid, we're also questioning the hidden ontology in classical (Einsteinian) epistemology that permeates Western thinking. This is the very ontology that is the basis for materialist theories that explain our state of being as distinct physical objects in a purely local universe.

And remember, a local universe is one of separation and not connection.

To wit: Bernard d'Espagnat[25], writing about interpretations of quantum theory, concluded that "The doctrine that the world is made up of objects whose existence is independent of human consciousness turns out to be in conflict with quantum mechanics and with facts established by experiment."

The challenge comes down to questioning an ontology based on an epistemology that has been proven to be invalid before we attempt to invalidate what we don't understand. The path is riddled with mental minefields. We are creatures with many attributes, some good, some not so good. In this instance, the most important one is a universal stubbornness to accept anything that doesn't fit the previous knowledge we've acquired through years of effort, study, more effort, and experience. None the less, all that education and experience has provided us with a set of subconscious presuppositions that shape every thought we have. If we are to learn more, that's the challenge we must face.

To begin a serious investigation, in the next chapter, we'll start with the definition of death. It is the most important starting point. Because the NDE is something that happens before the actual moment of *information-theoretic* death.[26] No Westerner knows what happens after.

I repeat, NDE's are not absolute proof of what happens after death. But some of them are absolute proof that the full range of consciousness is still an undefined attribute of sentient beings and we have not yet been able to describe all the possibilities.

In summary, we now understand the universe to be a very different place than we thought it to be. In this universe, the idea of a mechanistic reality that only conforms to a set of cause and effect calculations is obsolete. We are in constant interaction co-creating the reality we experience. It is no less real to us, but that reality is subjective. This places consciousness in a very different place, a primary place that offers us another avenue for exploring how it may function during an NDE. And in doing so, shed light on other Unexplained Consciousness Events.

Notes

Chapter 5

What is Death

"Life and death are one, even as the river and sea are one."

Khalil Gibran

All the experiences in the previous chapter were reported by people during stages in the process of dying. And because of this fact, the speculations in this book are limited to just that period when death seems to be imminent yet doesn't come. Also, because we are only interested in those subjective reports of events that can be validated intersubjectively[27] by others, we are dealing with only a small portion of the structure of an NDE.

These facts make the exact definition of death vital. In my opinion, even the use of the term, Near Death Experience, clouds up the issue. Therefore, I've used the term Unexplained Consciousness Events to make it abundantly clear that I am not focusing on all the other reported characteristics of NDE's, only those where a consciousness event could not be explained in any other way and was validated by at least one other person.

For instance, certain of the physiological effects of a "dying" brain, i.e., the tunnel and light, out of body experience, can all have scientifically explainable causes. Although they are important, these effects are not the topic of this book.

Death

Information theoretic death is the final stage when all bodily structures needed to form the personality are damaged beyond recovery. According to the current medical model of death, without the ability to reconstitute our personality we have lost the ability to be conscious and we are dead. But NDE's are causing us to re-think consciousness and specifically how it relates to the process of death and dying even though Western science claims that death is final.

Now some theoretical physicists and medical professionals are offering theories that have the potential to explain how forms of consciousness can continue after death. We can add this to the Buddhist literature on the process of death and dying and the continuation of consciousness in various forms. [28]

That said, in this chapter, we will explore a detailed definition of death and its relationship to consciousness from a Western perspective with a few simple references to Eastern thinking.

Until now we've defined death as the termination of the biological functions that sustain a living organism and, consequently, the end of consciousness. This definition implies consciousness is simply a function of our biology. There are other views beginning to get traction in Western thinking. As I pointed out before, philosopher of mind, David Chalmers, and others propose consciousness is a *non-reductive primitive*[29] more basic to the universe than matter and energy. Considering the proven fact that our consciousness consistently affects the outcomes of scientific experiments, this idea makes good sense.

History of Death

Until the last few decades, a simple definition of death has been sufficient in the West. For instance, most people don't know that in the "olden days" when an English sailor was sewn into his canvas hammock to be buried at sea, the last stitch was through his nose. That was the British Navy's way of being sure he was dead. Fortunately, that practice has been eliminated.

Since the development of modern medical techniques, we can bring people back from death as we understood it–as it was previously defined. Now, the actual moment of irreversible death is not as clear as we previously thought. Although, I doubt that many British sailors were committed to the deep alive.

It is interesting to note Buddhism practices a ritual based on a different belief about death. They consider death a process and its rituals are contained in what is commonly known as *The Tibetan Book of the Dead*, or *The Bardo Thodol: The Golden Opportunity of Death,* and assists the soul as it proceeds through the entire process of dying. This Tibetan text describes and is intended to guide one through the experiences one's consciousness has during and after death. The ritual is based on the belief our personal consciousness continues after death so that we can be reincarnated.

We are beginning to see as the Buddhists have known; death is a process, not merely an event. Given this discovery, this provides an interesting bridge between the thinking in Western and Eastern civilizations, even if we do not accept reincarnation.³⁰

Examples of *Dead* People Who Weren't Dead

"There are many anecdotal references to people being declared dead by physicians and then 'coming back to life,' sometimes days later in their own coffin, or when embalming procedures are about to begin […] much debate has taken place about the uncertainty of the signs of death.

"For example, people who have been stunned by significant electric shock or are found unconscious under icy water when given cardiopulmonary resuscitation (CPR) do survive, allowing an apparently dead person to come back.

"As medical technologies advance, ideas about when death occurs [are being] re-evaluated in light of the ability to restore a person to vitality after longer periods of apparent death had happened when CPR and defibrillation showed that cessation of heartbeat is inadequate as a decisive indicator of death. The lack of electrical brain activity may not be enough to consider someone scientifically dead."³¹

This last sentence has a direct bearing on the NDE's that are under consideration in this book.

Our Deepening Understanding of Death

"Therefore, the concept of *information theoretical* death has been suggested as a better means of defining when true death occurs. *Information-theoretic* death is the destruction of the human brain (or any cognitive structure capable of constituting a person) and the information within it to such an extent that recovery of the original person is theoretically impossible by any physical means.

"The concept of information-theoretic death arose in the 1990s in response to the problem that as medical technology advances, conditions previously considered to be death, such as cardiac arrest, become reversible and are no longer considered to be death. 'Information-theoretic death' is intended to mean a death that is absolutely irreversible by any technology, as distinct from clinical death and legal death, which denote limitations to contextually-available medical care rather than the true theoretical limits of survival".[32]

In the paper cited above, "Molecular Repair of the Brain", Ralph Merkle defined information-theoretic death as follows: "A person is dead according to the information-theoretic criterion if their memories, personality, hopes, dreams, etc. have been destroyed in the information-theoretic sense. That is, if the structures in the brain that encode memory and personality have been so disrupted that it is no longer possible in principle to restore them to an appropriate functional state, then the person is dead. If the structures that encode memory and personality are sufficiently intact that inference of the memory and personality are feasible in principle, and, therefore, restoration to an appropriate functional state is likewise feasible in principle, then the person is not dead.

"The exact timing of information-theoretic death is currently unknown. It has been speculated to occur gradually after many hours of clinical death at room temperature as the brain undergoes autolysis[33]. It can also occur more rapidly if there is no blood flow to the brain during life support, leading to the decomposition stage of brain death, or during the progression of degenerative brain diseases that cause extensive loss of brain structure".

Definition of Death Affects the Study of NDE's

The exact definition of death is vital to understand the subtle distinction between the state in which near death experiences happen, and the state of irreversible death. As I've shown, although there is a substantial, growing body of scientific literature on near death experiences, no verifiable record of anyone returning from an information-theoretic death to report his or her experiences is known in the West. However, there are accounts of the experience of death and reincarnation in Buddhist literature.[34]

So, it is in this larger context, we will examine reports on near death experiences and speculate about how these reports offer us interesting insights into the phenomenon of consciousness in the process leading up to and not ending in death and the possible functioning of consciousness in different forms.

Important Caveat

It is important to recognize that these events happen during the period preceding death while the individual is still alive. It is a somewhat grounded speculation, but none the less, a speculation that they continue after death.

In light of the above, the more recent explanations of death as a final cessation of all information-criteria functional capabilities, the primary question is: if the brain is the seat of our consciousness, how can we explain objectively verified NDE's if and when consciousness continues after all measurable brain functions have ceased?

Keep in mind here that the question refers to brains when functions seem to have ceased, but have not been damaged beyond recovery as in information-theoretic death. Also keep in mind that this question emerges from an Einsteinian (mechanistic) epistemology; the brain is a separate physical object in a local universe. We now know it is not.

In summary, we might still not yet understand death or the entire process of consciousness; in effect, the wholeness of life itself including how we fit in this universe.

In the Western model, our brains are separate organs in a body of many separate organs that is a distinct object in the universe. We now know we are not individual or distinct and are connected to and made up of quantum-entangled particles as is every other object in the universe. As a reminder: There are no isolated systems in the universe, which means our bodies and the area we call our brains emerge from and are connected to what we call objective reality. Our egos create the illusion we are separate and distinct – or better yet, as Einstein himself said, "separation is a delusion of our egos."

This discovery raises the question, knowing the brain is made up of quantum particles like all the rest of the universe, how can it create the consciousness required for it to exist per the Copenhagen Interpretation[35] of quantum mechanics? The brain cannot exist without someone or something consciously observing it. If it creates consciousness, how can it be the creator of itself to exist?

Relax, this is not an argument for a God or gods as the observer-creators. More to come on this topic.

Notes

Chapter 6

Where is Consciousness?

"There is only one unity, unified wholeness, total natural law, in the transcendental unified consciousness."

Maharishi Mahesh Yogi

Where is consciousness? It depends on who you ask: Although the different answers do emerge from a philosophical as well as scientific level. Most scientists and medical professionals will say it's in our brains. Most religionists will say it's in our souls. And this difference is the dichotomy between what philosophers call either monism or dualism.

As a reminder, monism is a theory or doctrine in philosophy that denies the existence of a distinction or duality, such as that between matter and mind, or God and the world. Dualism, in philosophy and theology, is any system that explains phenomena by two opposing principles. In simple terms, do we and the universe consist of one or two levels? For instance, in cosmology is there just the material world or does the supernatural exist too? In ontology, is to be human to have a material body only or do we also have souls? A tangent to this is the dualist, usually religious or (Cartesian) view that the soul is the basis of our consciousness.

These philosophical positions are the fundamental differences between scientific and religious philosophy. Many of the arguments between the two epistemological poles are based on this difference. And of course, much of the resistance, each to the other view, is based on this distinction.

For instance, the production theory of consciousness says it is an experience that the brain produces, and there is no other source. In other words, mind and matter are the same which is based on the monist view. Then there is the reduction or filtering view, which says the brain receives and filters information from a universal consciousness. This can also be based on the monist view, which in

69

my opinion differs from the traditional scientific monist view. (more to come later on this topic)

But the main question I'm asking is what is the effect these various views have on the potential for the mind and matter to be of one philosophical and scientific view?

The Scientific Unknown

There may be another way of exploring the question without the need to ground it in one or the other philosophical model. Both arguments exist in an incomplete contextual background. We know the atomic world, all the material, and energy we can identify is only about five percent of the total. The other 95 percent is unknown to us. We know it's there because we can measure its effects but we don't know what it is. We call it dark energy and dark matter.

The role of physicists is to point to the unknown, and they are pointing to 95 percent of the universe and saying we don't know what it is? This unknown is not driven by indifference, but by rigorous study. But the obvious point here is we live in a universe that we cannot fully describe with our previous models and our best mathematics.

Author, Chris Carter sums it up best, "It is remarkable that such ideas should arise from a study of the behavior of the most elementary of systems. That such systems point to a world beyond themselves is a fact that will be loved by all who believe that there are truths of which we know little, that there are mysteries seen only by mystics, and that there are phenomena inexplicable within our normal view of what is possible. There is no harm in this—physics indeed points to the unknown". (Carter, 2010)

So, while I can't prove it, nor can physics disprove it, it's entirely possible there's something going on here that might account for what some call consciousness or mind as separate from the brain. The key point is that we don't need to accept the existence of the soul or some other supernatural force to explain consciousness originating somewhere other than the brain. And we don't need to be dualists to suspect that the reduction or filtering concept of consciousness cannot exist within a monist scientific and philosophical framework.

This way we can open ourselves to both epistemologies of empiricism and rationalism to assist in understanding this mysterious phenomenon we call consciousness.

Is Consciousness in the Body?

In a previous chapter, it was suggested with the new meta-structure of knowledge placing consciousness at the foundation of the universe, we might consider that it permeates our whole body. For instance, we do know that our entire body is one big sensing instrument, so to speak. If this is so, then what is the relationship between our whole bodies and our consciousness? This question is provocative, but not new. As with every other new idea that promised to disrupt the status quo to place consciousness anywhere else is resisted by our need to maintain the coherency of our existing theory dependent models.

Further, the people who present the new and unusual are always considered with suspicion: heretics, so to speak. Nonetheless, throughout history, heretics have proposed disruptive new ideas that allowed us to make progress in our search for more knowledge. Some explanations of reality languished in the archives labeled as "heresies" for many years before they were accepted. To be sure, the question goes back a long way.

Historically speaking, the idea of a mind/body dualism goes at least as far back as Zarathustra.[36] Plato and Aristotle suggested the existence of an incorporeal soul. It was the seat of intelligence and wisdom. They believed that people's intelligence could not be explained by the functions of their physical body.

For centuries, the concept of the mind or soul was used to explain human consciousness. The soul has been an integral teaching in almost all religions. In most religious traditions, the soul is the conscious part of us that continues after our physical body dies.

In more recent times, this belief is disputed by most cognitive scientists, and especially by religious antagonists. Most of them believe we are born, we live, we die, the end. Even Stephen Hawking, the world-renown theoretical physicist recently weighed in with his opinion, "this is all there is."

Still, with all scientists now know about how our brains function physiologically, they cannot agree on an explanation of human consciousness, with or without the concept of a soul.

For instance, how does physical matter, like the substances in our brains, create something with no physical substance like our minds? At a deeper level, how does our mind, with no physical substance act on our body? And at an even deeper level how does our consciousness affect the quantum world when we produce the outcomes of our experiments by our methods of observation? We see it. We test it repeatedly. We prove it every time we test it. We still do not know the mechanism responsible.

At the human level, we understand the brain's electro-chemical functions very well. We've mapped it and know where actions are happening when we perform cognitive functions. But even as much as we know, no one can explain the essence of consciousness. We simply don't know what it is. Much like dark matter and energy, we know it's there because of its effects. But we don't have a universally agreed explanation for how immaterial consciousness works to effect material reality.

The famous double-slit experiment has is done thousands of times, and the result is always the same: The conscious act of measurement determines the outcome of the experiment. Light can be a wave or a particle depending on how we measure it. And this happens like a miracle with no obvious describable mechanism we know.

So, many scientists cannot empirically explain what they believe makes humans unique. Its effects are undeniably observable at the classical and quantum levels of reality. To repeat, the very attribute identified as uniquely human cannot be explained by the most highly regarded Western scientific methods of inquiry so far developed by humans–Western humans, that is.

What Might Consciousness Be?

To establish a baseline, let us start with a formal definition of consciousness: "Consciousness is variously defined as subjective experience, or awareness, or wakefulness, or the executive control system of the mind. It is an umbrella term that may refer to a variety of mental phenomena. Although humans realize what everyday experiences are, consciousness refuses to be defined, philosophers note. "Anything that we are aware of at a given moment forms part of our consciousness, making the conscious experience at once the most familiar and most mysterious aspect of our lives". (Schneider and Velmans 2007)

Also, it is subjective. We each know we are conscious, and think you are, but can never experience your consciousness the way you do. And you can never experience mine.

The concept of consciousness has not always been regarded as a legitimate area of scientific study. For most of humankind's existence, the question was already answered by religions. It resided in the soul, which was within the domain of religious explanations. Now the study of consciousness is on center stage of scientific investigations. The current study includes consciousness as mind, the brain, and how these processes interact to make us who we are as humans.

More relevant to our concerns in this book is the study of how our consciousness co-creates the reality we experience. The key point here is that our ontology and epistemology are fundamental to our present explanations of consciousness and how we resist learning more.

For instance, does our mind need a soul or can our body produce the mind without a soul? And to answer that question where do we look? The epistemology of empiricism or rationalism? This boils down to, do we look to scientific objectivity or do we honor subjective experience?

To paraphrase the evolutionary biologist, Richard Lewontin, when one restricts one's questions to a single domain where the source of knowledge is unchallenged, the answers will always be consistent with that ontology and epistemology.

For the scientist, an ontology based on empiricism is one kind of theory-based model of knowledge. For the religious believer, an ontology based on rationalism is another.

To a degree, the ontology of empiricism leads to what French-born American scholar and teacher, Jacques Barzun, describes as the "fallacy of believing that the method of science must be used on all forms of experience and, given time, will settle every issue." Good luck selling that idea to a devout religious believer.

In summary, this brings us once again to that all important issue, an explanation of the essence of our universe including how we interact with it. There are many schools of thought with competing propositions. As written above, the two most important divisions are monism and dualism. This is the question of whether the universe is a single material substance, monism, or dualistic, including either another natural level or a supernatural level. This question is particularly important as it relates to the questions of mind and consciousness.

Is consciousness an epiphenomenon[37] of the brain's processes? Is it an emergent property of biological, e.g., electrochemical functioning? Is it purely an epiphenomenon of a materialistic process, which would ground it in the monistic epistemology and ontology of empiricism? Or is it somehow non-material as the ancient scientist-philosophers believed and what our religious stories, even today, describe as our soul, which would ground it in dualism and rationalism? Once again, we can find better answers if we consider both.

Notes

Chapter 7

The Discovery of the Quantum Enters the Debate

"I read a book called 'The Tao of Physics' by Fritjof Capra that pointed out the parallels between quantum physics and Eastern mysticism. I started to feel there was more to reality than conventional science allowed for and some interesting ideas that it hadn't got around to investigating, such as altered states of consciousness".

Brian Josephson

Even with the discovery of the quantum level of the universe, scientific theories and many of our cognitive models are still based on Newtonian principles of a mechanical universe with Einsteinian enhancements. In other words, it is a deterministic mechanical place where distinct objects are separated by space, where cause and effect can be measured and anticipated with certainty based on predetermined calculations.

But this didn't make sense to many people even as early as the 1980's. "In 1986, Sir John Eccles[38] proposed that the probability of neurotransmitter release depended on quantum mechanical processes, which can be influenced by the intervention of the mind. This, Eccles said, provided the basis for the action of a free will". (Schwartz 2000)

It would seem free will could not come from deterministic mechanical processes. So how do we explain this paradox?

For instance, in the clockwork universe Newton described where every action and reaction can be predicted and explained mathematically, for free will to exist, determinism should not. In Newton's model, every physical action must be preceded by another physical cause; physical cause and physical effect, so to speak.

The Dreaded Interaction Problem

We know the mind is non-material, even if we accept that it is simply an epiphenomenon of the brain. So how does the non-material mind cause a material reaction in the brain resulting in a material action in the physical world? And if we could answer that question, it remains a mystery as to how our conscious attention can cause the outcomes of our scientific observations at the quantum level, e.g., the double slit experiment.

"Philosopher William Lycan calls this the "dreaded" interaction problem. How can something nonspatial, with no mass, location, or physical dimensions, possibly influence spatially bound matter? As K. R. Roa writes, the main problem with such dualism is the problem of interaction. How does unextended mind interact with the extended body? Any kind of causal interaction between them, which is presumed by most dualist theories, comes into conflict with the physical theory that the universe is a closed system and that every physical event is linked with an antecedent physical event. This assumption preempts any possibility that a mental act can cause a physical event". (Carter, 2010)

And even if we can ignore the unanswered question, in a deterministic universe, we would still not have free will. We would simply be automatons with limited options each time we acted. If you believe we are, you have company. Some philosophers still argue that we are automatons with limited options, but enough to cause us to believe we have free will.

There are those who believe because our choices seem infinite to us; we only think we have free will. This is an attempt to force fit a solution in defense of a deterministic, monist view of reality.

There are several theories more consistent with our current knowledge of the fundamental makeup of the cosmos. The one that fits best here is called, "Process Philosophy, which was developed by pioneer and English mathematician, Alfred North Whitehead, and is very consistent with Buddhist teachings about the goal of all meditation: the clear and penetrating awareness of change and impermanence; in effect, variability."[39]

This theory regards change as the cornerstone of reality. Taking this further into the philosophical, the Buddhist teaching of *impermanence* includes the Self. The key point being, "there is no permanent self." There is only the continually changing individual experience created by a confluence of multiple factors that make us who we are. Our egos create the illusion of self as separate from everything else, but we are always connected to the basic fabric of the universe.

"This view is strikingly consistent with recent developments in quantum physics." (Schwartz 2000) Although it proposes the essence of reality is its variability through change, Dualistic Interactionism is also consistent but not absolutely[40] the same as speculations in this book. It holds that consciousness and other aspects of mind occur interactively with our brains. Philosopher, Karl Popper, and Australian neurophysiologist, John Eccles, wrote: "the essential feature of dualistic interactionism is that the mind and brain are independent entities [...]and that they interact by quantum physics". (Schwartz 2000)

Dr. Rupert Sheldrake proposes that our minds are extended like energy fields around our bodies and consequently are related to but not being produced only by our brains.

If you are feeling confused at this point, you are in good company. There is another authentic position on consciousness called, "don't have a clue materialism." The people in this camp have simply given up trying to explain the mind or consciousness scientifically. But they do maintain it is a purely material phenomenon. To be clear, I think it can be purely materialistic and universal too.

So, are we left with this confusion or is there another way of explaining consciousness that can pull these arguments together in a rational and understandable way?

Another Promising View

Again, we back to Australian philosopher of mind, David Chalmers, who calls consciousness a non-reductive primitive, or a fundamental building block of reality, just as mass and energy, as well as space, are non-reductive primitives in scientific theories of the physical world. He takes consciousness as a primitive rather than as an emergent property of the physical brain. Another way of saying this is the brain emerges from consciousness and not vice versa. A view which is very consistent with what we find at the quantum level, in particular, the Copenhagen Interpretation of quantum mechanics.

He goes on to say, in this view, "mind is much more fundamental to the universe than we ordinarily imagine.[41] This theory has the added benefit of integrating mental events into the physical world. We need psychophysical laws connecting subjective experience to physical processes. Certain aspects of quantum mechanics lend themselves very nicely to this". (Schwartz 2000)

Theoretical physicist, Harry Stapp, has developed a complete model of how quantum action in the brain functions to facilitate physical actions at the classical level of reality. "According to his model, (and consistent with the Copenhagen Interpretation) if we intend to raise our arm, conscious observation collapses the wave functions of the calcium ions in our brains that are responsible for initiating the template to raise our arm." (Carter, 2010) (the parenthetical sentence added)

Theoretical biologist and M.D., Stuart Kauffman adds: "If quantum measurement is necessary for experiencing qualia, [42] then anesthetics may act by 'freezing' postsynaptic neurotransmitter receptors, perhaps in the post-synaptic membrane, into a stable classical state, such that they can no longer undergo measurement from quantum to classical, from Res Potentia to Res Extensa. Then experiences, qualia, cannot arise, and we are anesthetized". Dr. Stuart Hameroff, M.D., a practicing anesthesiologist of over 35 years agrees.

As I understand these men, when we are anesthetized, our conscious awareness is disconnected from interacting with the quantum level, Kaufman calls the poised realm. This says although the brain is Res Extensa (is real in a physical way) at the classical level it is temporarily *disengaged* from the mind and consciousness, which is consistent with Dr. Sheldrake's theory. (A key point here is that this is my speculation of Kauffman's, Hameroff's and Sheldrake's opinions and not meant to imply their agreement.) None the less, my speculation would only conceptually "disengage" the physical brain from the mind and consciousness.

Although we experience our physical bodies at the classical 3D level of reality we, brain included, our mind, and consciousness are part of, fully entangled with, and interacting at the quantum level. We are made of it.

In this way of thinking, we do have free will within the parameters of the natural laws of the universe. In other words, we can't just defy the law of gravity and decide to fly without the aid of a mechanical device.

As I've argued throughout this book, the blind spots of science and religion limit our ability to understand fully our reality. But we do get clues from time to time. Neither of these theory-based models of knowledge—social constructions—have enough common attributes to bridge rational discussion. Both will be closed to the other until we recognize their limitations of our knowledge of the universe. When we do, we open ourselves to the possibility that answers might exist in the 95 percent of the universe that science tell us is unknown to us.

Chalmers is philosophically proposing, and people like Kauffman, Hameroff, Sheldrake and Stapp are scientifically proposing the very platform that will allow reasonable dialogue: Chalmers' psychophysical laws, the open quantum system Kauffman calls the poised realm, Stapp's model of quantum actions at the cellular level of the brain, and Sheldrake's proposal that the mind is an extended energy field.

At this point, no models are complete, but our growing knowledge of the quantum level of our universe may create the bridge to develop and connect them. In the words of physicist Harry Stapp[43], "The replacement of the ideas of classical physics by the ideas of quantum physics completely changes the complexion of the mind-brain dichotomy, of the connection between mind and brain."[44]

To be clear, it changes this dichotomy because it explains that we, our brains, and everything else in the universe are of one substance. We are it, and it is us.

So, at a fundamental level what remains is the issue of dualism versus materialism. In my view, a different explanation of materialism seems to answer more questions. i.e., our reality is made up of one substance. Not the limited monistic materialism of scientific thinking that excludes anything not objectively explained at the classical level of the universe. Not the objective separated deterministic universe, but a naturalistic monism that includes other levels of reality we have not discovered yet and may never be able to experience from our classical 3D level.

Again, this is only my speculation, but it keeps the serious investigator out of the world of superstitious explanations. Maybe what some of us insist upon and call the supernatural realm is really an unperceived level of this mysterious universe.

In summary, we do not need dualism, the natural and supernatural, to explain the unexplainable. It is an artifact of a time when we did not have a deeper sense of how this universe works. It's possible that religious explanations of the soul were the only language we've had for describing something we intuitively know we have. Maybe the entire realm of religious explanation is based on our inability to know different levels of the universe directly. Now we can open our minds to new discoveries. If we do, I suspect we will find that death is simply a transformation?

To that end, the following chapters contain scientific facts, heresies, and some would claim fantasies. Whatever they are, they are designed to provoke new questions, not new answers. I offer them as just another opportunity to learn to live in the questions provoked by this mysterious cosmos. Although we may not like it, what seems like a paradox to us, may be the core logic of the universe.

Notes

Chapter 8

NDE's, Consciousness and the Quantum

"By studying thousands of detailed accounts of NDErs, I found evidence that led me to this astounding conclusion: NDE's provide such powerful scientific evidence that it is reasonable to accept the existence of an afterlife."

Jeffery Long, MD
Radiation oncologist, founder of Near Death Experience Research
Foundation (NDERF)

"In fact, a considerable body of credible evidence supports the probability of the post-death existence of consciousness and sentient future life continuity. First, it is the natural thing to expect since everything else in nature exhibits continuity through changes. Second, many credible witnesses report that they died and experienced certain adventures.

"Some died clinically and were revived. Some remember as children, details, and circumstances of former lives and some of their memories are corroborated by other people, standing up to the investigation of reputable researchers". (Thurman 1994)

Although these comments seem compelling, I remain a bit incredulous for reasons I have stated earlier: These people were not information-theoretic dead. Something about their reports leaves little doubt that there is much more here about consciousness we don't understand.

For those readers who may want to examine the full scope of NDE's, there are many books available that will explore the topic much more completely than this one. Many of them are listed in the bibliography. As we enter this chapter, remember we're looking at NDE's to study UCE's. Our topic is only that portion of an NDE when a veridical account of an unexplained consciousness event happens; something verified by other observers to be true.

Let's take a closer look.

Another reminder: A meta-structure is a foundation upon which a structure is built. At the beginning of the book, we compared two meta-structures and proposed how we need to move consciousness to the foundational level. Then we can begin to re-examine the ontological and epistemological models that form the theory of who we are and the knowledge we consider to be valid.

The interconnectedness of our prevailing ontology and epistemology has already been discussed. These are our explanations of our existence and our way of knowing them given our mostly unconscious insistence on clinging to a Newtonian model of a mechanistic universe. The key point here is that reconstruction can offer a new way of seeing what we call reality. By doing so, we can reorganize from the foundation up.

Another way of saying this is we may become different observers of the same reality, the reality that our original religions[45] tried to explain and science has tried to deny. If we do, we might create a new meaning of what we consider real. The key point here is the evidence may not change, but our interpretations may.

While reading the following, if you limit your interpretations to either one of the epistemological poles science or religion, your reactions may be, "it simply is not possible!" However, if you accept the validity of subjective experience reported in UCE's and specifically certain portions of NDE's as a subset, if you grasp how the universe functions at its most fundamental level, and if you don't just believe empirical evidence or religious mythology, you will be open to the purpose of this book; more questions and new discoveries that bring about more questions; and maybe the conversation for possibilities that I mentioned as a core reason for this book.

So, again, where is consciousness?

We know we are conscious. We know our brains do not have the physical capacity to produce our consciousness. Yet, we have it. In the present context, it would seem we are back to the old question about the faculty of mind or soul.

If we are new *observers* with new eyes, we might ask questions from a different ontological and epistemological foundation; develop a new story about what it means to be human and how we and our universe work together. Even as we approach this ancient question with new eyes, there are older theories that seemed to have been pointing in the right direction all along.

Collective unconscious is a term of analytical psychology, coined by Carl Jung: "It is a part of the unconscious mind, expressed in humanity and all life forms with nervous systems, and describes how the structure of the psyche autonomously organizes experience. Jung distinguished the *collective unconscious* from the *personal unconscious*, (Italics added) in that the personal unconscious is a personal reservoir of experience unique to each individual while the collective unconscious collects and organizes those personal experiences in a similar way with each member of a particular species".[46]

Jung stated, in his book *Archetypes and the Collective Unconscious*: "My thesis then, is as follows: in addition to our immediate consciousness, which is of a thoroughly personal nature and which we believe to be the only empirical psyche (even if we tack on the personal unconscious as an appendix), there exists a second psychic system of a collective, universal, and impersonal nature which is identical in all individuals. This collective unconscious does not develop individually but is inherited. It consists of pre-existent forms, the archetypes, which can only become conscious secondarily and which give definite form to certain psychic contents.

"The archetypes form a dynamic substratum common to all humanity, upon the foundation of which each individual builds his own experience of life, developing a unique array of psychological characteristics. Thus, while archetypes themselves may be conceived as a relative few innate nebulous forms, from these may arise innumerable images, symbols, and patterns of behavior. While the emerging images and forms are apprehended consciously, the archetypes which inform them are elementary structures which are unconscious and impossible to apprehend".[47]

Some thought Jung's theories to be pseudoscientific in the early days of his work. Now, we may consider them to be prescient because of scientific discoveries. If we were to reconstruct Jung's concepts of the collective unconscious and the personal unconscious in more scientific terms, we might speculate he was pointing to something very real.

These proposals are not that different from Buddhist theories about the distinction between gross consciousness[48] and subtle consciousness[49].

Cognitive scientists Lakoff and Johnson propose that all thought is embodied. That is, our bodies contain it. But there is a problem with this proposition. There is evidence to the contrary as demonstrated by Simon Berkovitch, Roger Penrose, and Dutch neurobiologist, Herms Romijn, (i.e., our brains cannot work fast enough). Which leaves the unanswered question in Western thinking: where are the personal and collective unconscious located, if not in our brains?

Eastern thinking seems to deal with this question without the need to place the whole consciousness process in our brains by making the distinction between our gross bodies and our subtle bodies.

Roger Penrose, a quantum physicist, offers a clue with his theory of consciousness explained by connecting it to the quantum level. Understanding the details of quantum mechanics is a rigorous process that confuses even well-educated scientists. But even a layperson can see that consciousness is somehow determining the results of our observations as in the double slit experiment, and there is no scientifically identified way of explaining how.

We're told that our brains don't have the capacity to produce the total consciousness experience. Somehow, consciousness is present and necessary to produce the outcomes of our scientific experiments and what we call our subjective experience. So, if it so difficult to understand, why do we have such resistance to documented verifiable clues to the authenticity and substance of consciousness continuing during near death experiences (NDE's), not to mention all the other forms of UCE's

Once again, we're back to our presuppositions based on the Newtonian mechanistic view of how the universe works and how our brains are separate objects living in disconnected physical entities called individual human beings. Nothing can be further from the truth.

Another Meta-structure

Caveat: I am not a qualified scientist and have not had a direct experience of an NDE. Although I have had many conversations with people who've experienced UCE's, my *research* is limited to the literature about NDE's, and not a direct examination of these cases. What follows is offered to simply provoke questions, not as conclusive proof. Remember, what we do know for sure is scientific investigation leaves what is called the *residual ten percent.* It is this unexplained ten percent that falls outside of our logical axioms and opens the door to new discoveries.

Research scientists and physicians are making new discoveries every day. We know the brain dies at final information theoretic death. Consciousness cannot be found in our brain's processes even when we are alive. Now, we know our brain does not even have the physical capacity to produce or contain our consciousness. All this said, the accounts of certain NDE's below offer a specific perspective on the general category of UCE's for the reader's consideration. They can be best appreciated on the proposed new underlying knowledge meta-structure with consciousness at the base.

Our current system of knowledge is based on the meta-structure illustrated earlier as a pyramid. As a reminder, it started with its foundation in physics at the bottom which then led up to chemistry which led to biology which led to psychology which leads to our explanations of consciousness.

In this model, we think of the brain as the seat of consciousness, and we think of it as physically separate and distinct from the universe. Consequently, NDE's are difficult to accept if the brain is inactive and disconnected from the universe. But if we think of ourselves as spatial extensions, features of the universe as we and the universe emerge from consciousness, it allows us to consider NDE's as another form of conscious manifestation. In doing so, we open the door to seeing other UCE's as manifestations of our whole body's entanglement with all the universe and its unexplained features that seem so remote in a mechanistic model.

As you saw, the new knowledge meta-structure would then place consciousness at the bottom of the pyramid such that physics, chemistry, biology, and psychology as bodies of human knowledge emerge out of universal consciousness. Excuse the spiritual sounding analog, but this suggests that the universe is more like a gigantic thought than a large machine. I'm not alone in that idea.

In summary, a speculation: We, our brains, and everything else emerges out of a universal consciousness, and our brains are not the only way of being connected to it. We are immersed in it. We are made of it. We are in it and never separate from it. Keep this interconnectedness in mind as you read the following accounts of NDE's in the next chapter.

Notes

Chapter 9

Selected Cases of NDE's

"Death is a metamorphosis of time – one more illusion born of our mental concepts."

Jeffery Long, MD

"The content of an NDE and the effects on patients seem similar worldwide, across all cultures and times. The subjective nature and absence of a frame of reference for this experience lead to individual, cultural, and religious factors determining the vocabulary used to describe and interpret the experience. NDE's can be defined as the reported memory of the whole of impressions during a special state of consciousness, including a number of special elements such as out-of-body experience, pleasant feelings, seeing a tunnel, light, deceased relatives, or a life review". (Van Lommel 2007)

As we would expect, there is a large body of scientific and religious repudiations claiming these experiences are a natural physiological phenomenon, hysteria, or simply a hoax. Nonetheless, there are certain aspects of these experiences that make them difficult to dismiss, even by the most skeptical researcher. The following accounts are from people who have had experiences not readily explainable by the medical profession or the existing system of scientific or religious logic.

Case One

"There is a well-documented report of a patient with the constant registration of the EEG during surgery for a gigantic aneurysm at the base of the brain, operated with a body temperature between 10 and 15 degrees Celsius. She was connected to a heart-lung machine, with VF, with all blood drained from her head, with a flat line EEG, with clicking devices in both ears, with eyes taped shut, and this patient experienced an NDE with an out-of-body experience, and all details she perceived and heard could later be verified." (Van Lommel 2007)

More about this case follows: Dr. Michael Sabom is a cardiologist whose latest book, Light, and Death, includes a detailed medical and scientific analysis of an amazing near-death experience of a woman named Pam Reynolds.

She underwent a rare operation to remove a giant basilar artery aneurysm in her brain that threatened her life. The size and location of an aneurysm, however, precluded its safe removal using the standard neurosurgical techniques.

She was referred to a doctor who had pioneered a daring surgical procedure known as a hypothermic cardiac arrest. It allowed Pam's aneurysm to be excised with a reasonable chance of success. This operation, nicknamed "standstill" by the doctors who perform it, required that Pam's body temperature be lowered to 60 F degrees, her heartbeat and breathing stopped, *her brain waves flattened*, and the blood drained from her head. In everyday terms, she was put to death. After removing the aneurysm, she was restored to life.

During the time that Pam was in standstill, she experienced an NDE. Her remarkably detailed veridical out-of-body observations during her surgery were later verified to be very accurate. This case is considered to be one of the strongest cases of veridical evidence in NDE research because of her ability to describe the unique surgical instruments and procedures used and her ability to describe in detail these events while she was clinically and brain dead.

"When all of Pam's vital signs were stopped, the doctor turned on a surgical saw and began to cut through Pam's skull. While this was going on, Pam reported that she felt herself "pop" outside her body and hover above the operating table. Then she watched the doctors working on her lifeless body for a while. From her out-of-body position, she observed the doctor sawing into her skull with what looked to her like an electric toothbrush. Pam heard and reported later what the nurses in the operating room had said and exactly what was happening during the operation. At this time, every monitor attached to Pam's body registered "no life" whatsoever. (Sabom 1998)

Although Ms. Reynolds's story and Dr. Sabom's analysis seems clear to the layperson, Dr. Kevin Nelson, neurologist, in his book, *The Spiritual Doorway in the Brain*, has this to say: "Pam's was a real, profoundly important spiritual experience. But it falls short of scientific proof that consciousness transcends the material world." (Nelson 2011)

Considering Dr. Nelson's very qualified professional opinion, keep in mind consciousness might not need to transcend the material world for such an experience to be real. Consider, what if the material world emerges from consciousness and functions in the natural world in ways that cannot be described with our present day scientific models? Again, consider Dr. David Chalmers' suggestion that consciousness is a non-reducible primitive in the universe at the same level of matter and energy.

In other words, even if this woman could not possibly have consciously—in a traditional sense—experienced what she could describe in detail after her recovery, a traditional sense is limited by the presuppositions that inform our traditions: the existing knowledge meta-structures.

Case Two

In another instance: "During the night shift, an ambulance brings in a 44-year old cyanotic, comatose man into the coronary care unit. He was found in a coma about 30 minutes before in a meadow. When we go to intubate the patient, he turns out to have dentures in his mouth. I remove these upper dentures and put them onto the "crash cart." After about an hour and a half, the patient has sufficient heart rhythm and blood pressure, but he is still ventilated and intubated, and he is still comatose.

"He is transferred to the intensive care unit to continue the necessary artificial respiration. Only after more than a week do I meet again with the patient, who is by now back on the cardiac ward. The moment he sees me, he says: 'Oh, that nurse knows where my dentures are.' I am very surprised. Then he elucidates: "You were there when I was brought into the hospital, and you took my dentures out of my mouth and put them onto that cart, it had all these bottles on it and there was this sliding drawer underneath, and there you put my teeth." I was especially amazed because I remembered this happening while the man was in deep coma and in the process of CPR.

"It appeared that the man had seen himself lying in bed, that he had perceived from above how nurses and doctors had been busy with the CPR. He was also able to describe correctly and in detail the small room in which he had been resuscitated as well as the appearance of those present like myself. He is deeply impressed by his experience and says he is no longer afraid of death." (Van Lommel 2007)

Case Three

And another: "During my cardiac arrest I had an extensive experience, and later I saw, apart from my deceased grandmother, a man who had looked at me lovingly, but whom I did not know. More than ten years later, at my mother's deathbed, she confessed to me that I had been born out of an extramarital relationship, my father being a Jewish man who had been deported and killed during the second World War, and my mother showed me his picture. The unknown man that I had seen more than ten years before during my NDE turned out to be my biological father." (Van Lommel 2007)

Remember, although one might argue this phenomenon is evidence of a supernatural world, I disagree. My premise is that what we have explained as supernatural for all history might simply be another element of the natural world we are just now beginning to probe with Western science.

Reconsider here Dr. Shushan's comprehensive research in ancient religious formations across cultures, languages, and geographically distant regions of the world. And how there is compelling evidence that points to NDE's as the reason for the human religious belief in an afterlife. Other cultures are full of explanations, traditions, and poetics pointing to different levels of reality. The one thing they're free of is the insistence of Western science that its theories and model will explain everything.

The explanations, whether they be natural or supernatural, become less important when we consider the effect NDEs have on those who recall them. As a prime and relevant example to those of us who are Christians, remember the dramatic transformation of the persecutor Saul of Tarsus to disciple St. Paul.

From Pim van Lommel, "Nearly all people who have experienced an NDE lose their fear of death. This is due to the realization that there is a continuation of consciousness, even when you have been declared dead by bystanders or even by doctors. You are separated from the lifeless body, retaining the ability of perception. It is outside my domain to discuss something that can only be proven by death. For me, however, the experience was decisive in convincing me that consciousness lives on beyond the grave. Death was not death, but another form of life.

"This experience is a blessing for me, for now, I know for sure that body and mind are separated and that there is life after death. Following an NDE people know of the continuity of their consciousness, retaining all thoughts and past events. And this insight causes exactly their process of transformation and the loss of fear of death. Man appears to be more than just a body". (Van Lommel 2007)

Not all people who have NDEs report these kinds of experiences. However, enough people across all cultures do, and this must offer us an opportunity to understand better the nature of human existence and how we interact with our universe.

There is a bonus here: The patients who remembered NDEs had new insights they shared: "their insight into what is important in life had changed: love and compassion for oneself, for others, and for nature. They now understood the cosmic law that everything one does to others would ultimately be returned to oneself: hatred and violence as well as love and compassion. Remarkably, there was often evidence of increased intuitive feelings. Furthermore, the long-lasting transformational effects of an experience that lasts only a few minutes was a surprising and unexpected finding". (Van Lommel 2007)

(Remember St. Paul's experience that mentioned earlier)

Science and religion can only answer the questions raised by these experiences if they are willing to challenge the epistemologies that inform them. In other words, allow that there are other ways of knowing what we know, which are equally as valid and should be taken into consideration.

What About Fake Reports of NDE's?

As you would expect, the publicity about these experiences has spawned fake stories now being debunked with scientifically objective methods, the same methods being used to qualify those that are authentic.

Even with some fake reports, the growing body of evidence cannot be denied nor can it be fully investigated by the scientific or religious communities unless they remove the barriers of previous suppositions. They do not allow the necessary questions to be asked and would not accept the validity of the answers. In simple terms, the objective methods of scientific investigation cannot explain a person's subjective experience. And thousands of years of religious mythology can best be understood as authentic efforts to explain the unexplainable; in many instances, figuratively accurate but not literally true.

We do know when a person is completely (information theoretic) dead, we cannot bring this individual back to life. We also know in some instances we can bring them back from the beginning process we call clinical death (i.e., when classical life functions seem to be ended). This issue seemingly points to a limitation in the argument for the authenticity of NDEs. And I do agree this is a limitation.

The counter-argument against NDEs is subtle. Is the NDE experience something limited to the biological *process* of dying? We still cannot speak with the complete assurance it will continue after final death occurs (although Buddhist literature describes the stage between death and rebirth, called the *Bardo* or the *betweens*).

These questions and others have created a new area of interest for medical science. Is death the end of life and personal consciousness? Or is it a transition to another natural state of being? Fortunately, some advanced-thinking scientific and medical professionals are taking these questions seriously with no small risk to their reputations. These are the people who can accept the different meta-structure I've referred to throughout this book. A meta-structure that allows for the serious investigations of those very real phenomena that seem to fall outside our current modes of investigation.

In summary, we are in a very interesting time. We are now investigating other phenomenon, as well as NDEs that are not explainable in our classic systems of logic. We are forced to become different observers just to allow that what we are now finding is undeniably inconsistent with our premises. As noted repeatedly: our scientific common sense is no longer exclusively valid.

In other words, our questions regarding what have been to date, metaphysical mysteries, may be revealing themselves in scientific discoveries. Our religions are based on primitive explanations of our world, and our science is based on "human experience…a misleading guide to the true nature of reality". What better answers might we develop with our newfound discoveries if, and when, we become different observers?

Notes

Chapter 10

Delving Deeper

"If the discovery of the quantum level of the universe has done nothing else, it has shaken classical physics loose from its foundations. In doing so, we now know that the universe is of one substance, coherent and non-local. We can no longer use classical physics as the basis for our illusions of separation".

—Charles Eisenstein
Speaker, writer

Since the early 1900s, physicists had to create a whole new system of logic based on the discovery of the quantum because classical scientific logic was not able to explain what was found at the elemental level of the universe. Only a new set of quantum laws can resolve several, seemingly mysterious problems, and explain new data at the subatomic level.

The perplexing problem is the universe seems to work per two different conflicting sets of natural laws. This finding defied our existing logic; specifically, the determinism embodied in the Aristotelian logic of the excluded middle, i.e., either A or not A, and added a new dimension to conflicts with the Cartesian dualist nature of mind and body. Nevertheless, the universe seems to work according to two different schemes.

Several theories have since evolved as attempts to reconcile the question: how does the universe work according to two different conflicting sets of laws? Still incomplete, one of the theories to evolve from this question is the *superstring theory*.[50] Another is supersymmetry or SUSY, and another M-theory. At the most fundamental level, the simple explanation is, the universe is operating according to one set of laws, and there is a unified landscape of vibrating strings of energy, in superposition, [51] which requires ten dimensions[52] in space-time to exist. Given each string's vibration frequency, it will become a part of different particle fields of energy.

This is an oversimplification of a complex theory with several variations. Briefly, this theory tries to unify the four forces, electromagnetism, gravity, the strong and weak (nuclear forces), and all of what seem like the fundamental material elements of the universe coming from a single unified field of vibrating dimensionless strings. There are several types of these strings that all into various classes. This theory opens the door just a bit to explaining how the two different conflicting sets of natural laws at work in the universe could come from one underlying principle. It is important to note these theories are very difficult to understand. To wit: From a lecture by theoretical physicist and proud heretic, Freeman Dyson:

"The main thing which I am trying to suggest by this discussion is the extreme remoteness of the superstring from any objects which we can see and touch. Even for experts in theoretical physics, superstrings are hard to grasp. Theoretical physicists are accustomed to living in a world which is removed from tangible objects, at least, two levels of abstraction. From tangible atoms, we move by one level of abstraction to invisible fields and particles.

"A second level of abstraction takes us from fields and particles to the symmetry groups by which fields and particles are related. The superstring theory takes us beyond symmetry groups to two further levels of abstraction. The third level of abstraction is the interpretation of symmetry groups in terms of ten-dimensional space-time.

"The fourth level is the world of superstrings by whose dynamical behavior the states are defined. It is no wonder that most of us had a hard time trying to follow Ed Witten[53] all the way to the fourth level." (Dyson 1988)

Underlying all this discussion is the relevant finding to this inquiry: at the most fundamental level of our Universe, there is only a landscape of probability, where everything exists in a state called *superposition*[54]. There is no certainty there. Something becomes certain (i.e., from all possibilities to a single position, place, and time) when observation reduces it; in other words, it is measured.

This process is what Roger Penrose[55] calls: objective reduction. It brings something into the *actual* level of the universe from the level called the *probable*. The observers collapse the probability waves and create the outcome by the act of observation thereby causing a particle to take a definite position from the possibility of all positions. The effect does not happen until the observer looks for it. When we do this, we are causing the effect we observe. In Einstein's words, "it spatially extends" into the 3D classical level of reality from a bubbling foam of probability waves and becomes actual. Mysteriously, yet a scientifically proven fact, this is all done with our consciousness by some mechanism we cannot explain using our current scientific methods.

In other words, it moves from the quantum space of pure probability to the actual world we experience simply by conscious observation.[56] We might find an analogy in psychiatrist Carl Jung's belief that the bases of our reality originate outside the world of our senses. In other words, he believed that they exist independently of the world we know. Further, he posited that they are known directly by our minds.

It's conscious agents all the way down

We are the individual conscious agents who create our reality and we have lots of company. It is clearly understood by those most familiar with the quantum laws upon which the universe functions that we simply cannot experience reality as it is. Evolution has adapted us to fit the environment we inhabit. The operative word here is "fit." We only perceive what provides us the best fit to our circumstances. More precisely we are the conscious agents who create our subjective experience by observing only that portion of reality we need to function.

For one example, we live in a sea of electromagnetic radiation, only a portion of which we are consciously aware. We can see some colors and we can hear some sounds without the aid of our artificial devices. Yet birds can perceive certain magnetic forces and use them for navigation over long distances because they've evolved to fit their ecological niche,

Our internal reality we can sense, (see, hear, feel, taste, etc.) is a creation of our central nervous systems. Our external social reality is co-created with other human beings. In addition to that created by other human beings, much of the external physical reality is co-created with other sentient beings. For instance, insects and birds co-create portions of reality that are out of our reach yet must exist for the whole web of life to survive. This says that consciousness is not limited to human beings. Every living being is involved in co-creating life on this planet.

Every life form in the chain of life that started with the first living cells and evolved to the millions of life forms today must have had some level of consciousness to co-create the niches they occupy. Without every one of those niches, we humans wouldn't be here. I would not have written this and you would not be reading it.

So, our consciousness depends on all the previous forms to exist. Think about this observation when you read about another threatened species about to become extinct or the damage we are doing to the entire web of life, of which we are a part.

Much to Absorb

Even Einstein himself struggled with the quantum mechanics that underlies all of reality. He refused to believe that the moon wasn't there when he didn't look at it. Yet per the Copenhagen Interpretation[57], it wouldn't be there if he didn't observe it. This makes more sense if we restate it this way; in fact, it wouldn't be there <u>for him</u> because he creates his own "objective" reality. There is only our personal subjective reality that we call objective reality, as we observe the world around us. So, every personal act of observation creates the personal result of that observation.

Until we create our personal subjective experience and co-create our shared seemingly objective experience, there is only a coherent fabric of probability waves upon which we can build that experience. Waves like those we find in the double slit experiments that become actual particles when we measure them.

Consciousness creates the universe as we experience it. That is scientific fact. What remains are the questions, is that consciousness pervasive throughout the universe? And if it is, how do we interact with it in this act of co-creation?

In summary, if we stretch our imagination by connecting the quantum system and the Cartesian concept of a "brain—mind" dichotomy, this proposition might be consistent with David Chalmers' proposal that consciousness is a non-reductive primitive in the physical makeup of the universe.

As importantly, it raises this question into clearer focus. Does the brain, as separate from the mind, works as a kind of reduction filter for protecting us from cosmic overload on our central nervous system? Does it take a functioning brain to negotiate an entangled universe of pure probabilities and create the illusion that we are time-bound individuals separated from it all in each passing moment?

Remember, the result of evolution is to create the best fit. That doesn't mean it allows us full access to how the actual universe is. The full experience of the universe as it is lies beyond our ability to perceive it with our current capabilities. While this fact should jolt us into a different paradigm of awareness, it also offers us exciting possibilities for exploration and learning.

Notes

Chapter 11

Time, the Brain, and Their Implications

"If that reality encompasses all the events in space-time, the total loaf exists. Just as we envision all of space really being out there, as really existing, we should also envision all of time as really being out there, as really existing too. The only thing that's real is the whole picture of space-time."

Brian Greene, Theoretical Physicist

You might be asking what has time to do with NDE's, consciousness, and the quantum. Let's start by considering Einstein's theory of special relativity. It is another view from classical physics to be considered in this effort to understand NDE's. It is the theory that forms the concept of space-time[58]. He proved space and time are unified, which makes time a fourth dimension. We now understand we can experience three spatial dimensions and a fourth temporal dimension, time. Our understanding of time is somehow created by and limited to us while we experience life here at the classical 3D level, the one we call reality. Time is an illusion of our consciousness and doesn't exist at the quantum level.

Remember the description of an NDE about these seemingly contradictory concepts of time: "A woman who was struck by a car wrote (of her NDE): It was only different in the sense that it was another space and another perception of being – I believe there was an all around awareness that didn't require thought in the way that our minds—brains rather – are programmed and designed to register them. This is beyond the speed of light if you will". (Long 2010)

Greene's description in an earlier quote and this woman's account brings us to a difficult phenomenon to explain. In the experience in our 3D actual world, we are conscious of sequential time—from the past to present to future. But in the basic or fundamental level of the universe, the one that gives rise to our experience of reality here at the classical level, the space-time loaf is frozen and can be experienced asymmetrically; past and future. Somehow people who report NDE's experience time in this way.

Verbatim reports of NDE's as they compare to scientific descriptions of the universe:

"Space and time are illusions that hold us to our physical realm; out there all is present simultaneously." (from Beverly Brodsky's near-death experience, 1970)

"During this experience, time had no meaning. Time was an irrelevant notion. It felt like an eternity. I felt like I was there an eternity." (from Grace Bubulka's near-death experience, 1988?)

"I didn't know if I had been in that light for a minute of a day or a hundred years." (from Jayne Smith's near-death experience, 1965?)

"Earthly time had no meaning for me anymore. There was no concept of "before" or "after." Everything - past, present, future - existed simultaneously." (from Kimberly Sharp's near-death experience, date unknown)

"Time could also be contracted, I found. Centuries would condense into seconds. Millenniums would shrink into moments. The entire civilization that I was part of passed by in the blink of an eye." (from John Star's near-death experience, date unknown)

"Time and space, as we know them, exist only on the Earth realm. When you leave the Earth realm, you leave such constraints." (from P.M.H Atwater's Beyond the Light)

"And there are probably other, better examples from other near-death experiences. So, what does this prove? Absolutely nothing. What does this imply? A great deal.

"I find it difficult to accept that the above observations about time and space could have been generated by a malfunction of the right temporal lobe distorting these people's time sense as some have suggested. In particular, Jeanie Dicus' comment is downright astonishing. Compare her statement to this quote:

"...time is an illusion. The phenomena from which we deduce its existence are real, but we interpret them wrongly..."[59]

Even at our level of reality, events can be experienced by one person as something that happened already and for another as something yet to happen. In other words, our experience of time is relative to each of us and consequently individuals can experience the same events at different times. Although our consciousness tells us time only moves forward, this is one of the limitations that adapts us to fit our reality.

Theoretical physicist, Marcelo Gleiser explains our inability to see the true nature of reality this way: "If we could wear glasses with the prescription that the theory of relativity dictates, we would see the union of space and time in all its glory... Picturing space-time as a rubber sheet again, at the quantum level we would see oscillations that twist and contort it in myriad ways. Time runs amok. The consequences are mind-boggling. Without reliable measures of distance and time, or how to interpret them probabilistically, the whole edifice of physics crumbles."

How did Einstein figure this out? Well, we know at our level, the classical level of the universe, the maximum speed of light is 299,338 meters (186,000 miles) per second. The speed of light is constant no matter what the circumstances or who measures it. For this to be true, space must expand and contract. And for this to be true, space and time must be unified into what we call space-time.

In addition to our inability to perceive the whole of space-time as it is, we have another limitation to consider. And that is, how the brain is not able to produce the consciousness of those reported by people during NDE's. To wit: As we will see, the brain, as a closed system capable of internal and consistent computations, is not only unable to experience the reality the woman quoted above did, it's also insufficient to elicit human consciousness.

Our Not So Speedy Brain

Researchers have tried to create artificial intelligence with computer technology, hoping to simulate programs evoking consciousness. Quantum physicist, Roger Penrose, argues that algorithmic computations cannot simulate mathematical reasoning. "Penrose offers an [another] quantum mechanical hypothesis to explain the relationship between consciousness and the brain. And Simon Berkovitch, a professor in Computer Science of the George Washington University, has calculated that the brain has an absolutely inadequate capacity to produce and store all the informational processes of all our memories with associative thoughts.

We would need 1024 operations per second, which is absolutely impossible for our neurons. Herms Romijn, a Dutch neurobiologist, comes to the same conclusion. One should conclude that the brain has not enough computing capacity to store all the memories with associative thoughts from one's life, has not enough retrieval abilities, and seems not to be able to elicit consciousness." (Van Lommel 2007)

So, we now have two confounding variables: (1) Time as we know it doesn't exist at the quantum level, even though our perception of it does at the classical level. (2) And our physical brains at the classical 3D level cannot work fast enough to create conscious thought.

How is this possible? If our connection to reality must be faster than our brains can function while we are here in this 3D space-time, and a person's experience can be instantly whole and complete during an NDE, something other than our brain is at work.

These emerging discoveries are pointing to something very interesting in this regard. They suggest our minds are not limited by the laws of classical physics as are our brains. Remember Sheldrake's proposal that our minds are energy fields that extend beyond our brains and bodies.

Our thoughts can emerge much faster than our brains can function. How is this possible if our minds are simply an epiphenomenon of our brains? And even more mysteriously, how can our brain even exist if only measurement or observation can bring the probability of its existence into reality? Is it able to observe itself? Is something else observing it? Or does it exist only as a human concept until it's directly observed by a physician or scientist? If we take the Copenhagen interpretation to the logical conclusion, there is no distinct physical object in space until it is observed, not even a brain. This dilemma is what theoretical physicist Amit Goswami refers to as the *tangled hierarchy* of our brain function where the "observer is the observed and vice versa."

Donald D. Hoffman, a professor of cognitive science at the University of California, Irvine offers this opinion, "I think that's absolutely true. The neuroscientists are saying, "We don't need to invoke those kind of quantum processes, we don't need quantum wave functions collapsing inside neurons, we can just use classical physics to describe processes in the brain. I'm emphasizing the larger lesson of quantum mechanics: Neurons, brains, space … these are just symbols we use; they're not real. It's not that there's a classical brain that does some quantum magic. It's that there's no brain!"

Do we not have brains?

Quantum mechanics says that classical objects—including brains—don't exist independently of an observer. Well, we do know we have thoughts, and we do know that a brain exists when we observe it. And we know we have what we call minds, that ethereal non-physical experience where our thoughts happen instantly and discontinuously, leaping from one topic to another. Yet if we want to process a thought more thoroughly, it takes longer. Why the difference in speed? Do our minds work at quantum speed and our brains take longer to process information? I know it seems like a strange question because I just pointed out that per quantum mechanics, we don't have a brain, at least until someone observes it.

Even limited by our language restrictions, scientists are continuing to find evidence for the biological *brain* mechanisms (that part of our bodies) at work as we interact with the quantum level. If we rephrase that statement to reflect the fact that we don't truly have these linguistically defined bodily distinctions, (more to come on this topic in the next chapter) we could say that scientists are finding evidence for how we as biological spatial extensions interact with the quantum level from which we emerge and are a part. Does this say we and our minds are separate but connected in ways we simply do not understand? Or are they the same thing? Have we simply separated them conceptually because we can't understand how they truly work?

Maybe we're confusing the limitations of our language with the limitations of our human capacities. When we insist that the linguistically defined area of our body called the brain is the seat of all forms of consciousness, we are creating artificial limitations that reflect our inability to understand the fullness of human possibilities. The ideological limitations of science and religion give us the patina of authority to end the discussion, thereby reinforcing our assurance that we know what there is to know about how we function.

Sorry folks, it's just not true. We simply do not fully understand the processes of our body, mind, and consciousness. Our discovery of how the universe functions at the quantum level *without time* when our consciousness interacts with it *in time* simply won't let us end the discussion where we are.

If we leave it at the classical 3D level, we have all three components, brain, mind, and consciousness existing in time. But that's only part of the story. How we understand time being different at the classical and the quantum levels, don't allow us to think of all three existing in the same space. Yet they must interact in ways that we don't yet understand. A good example is that most NDEr's tell us how they're affected by a difference in how they experience time.

Time and Whole Life Reviews

As an example of this time variation, whole life reviews are a consistently reported experience in NDEs, and the descriptions are all similar: They happen instantly and "holistically." We know time is a function of our experience only at the classical level of the universe. Our experience of time does not exist at the quantum level. It starts when something is measured or observed and becomes actual at our classical 3D level.

There may be a clue in what Penrose and Romijn cited above: "The phase speed in this invisible and non-measurable phase-space varies from the speed of light to infinity, while the speed of particles in our manifest physical real-space varies from zero to the speed of light. The phase-space generates events that can be located in our space-time continuum, the manifest world, or real-space. Everything visible emanates from the invisible." (Van Lommel 2007)[60]

It is interesting to note all human explanations of heaven, paradise, or nirvana considered them to be *invisible and in another dimension.* In effect, this scientific theory hypothesizes and religious stories provide a practical framework for all of the reported experiences of NDEs; continuity of consciousness, whole life reviews, meeting deceased loved ones, no fear of death, a full comprehension of the true meaning of life and in some instances by having access to the universal cosmic consciousness – all of the knowledge in the universe.

And all this happens when that gray matter we call our brains is not functioning during an NDE. When that one area of our whole body is not working as it should, it does not cancel out the rest, unless we want to think it does because science, the very body of knowledge that is limited to understanding only 5 percent of the universe, tells us so.

Maybe our search area is too small, and our language is too limited. After all, our body is made up of so much more than that small area we call our brain. Maybe we're not limited by our earth-bound concept and experience of time. Maybe that's an effect of an evolutionary fit "brain" as it receives and filters information that would make us fully aware of the universe and how it functions, but overwhelm us in the process. Then might we describe the NDEr's experience as an unbounded awareness by a different kind of observer not dependent only on their "brain"?

Escaping the bonds

Do these people experience an unbounded awareness because, during an NDE, they are not physiologically space, time, and ego-bound by what the Buddhists call our gross consciousness? Are they unified because their subtle consciousness is in contact with the cosmological unity of our universe, as described by the same Buddhist theories? Buddhist descriptors are here, not as complete explanations but only to point to centuries of study in Eastern tradition. In other words, these are not the inventions or the ramblings of a layman's understanding of the scientific material.

This is the very experience described to us by all the great prophets of our world. This is the goal of all enlightenment. This is the goal of the deepest forms of meditation and prayer. This is the power of our minds, not our brains. Of course, these are my speculations based on certain factual scientific discoveries and mathematically-proven principles. They are speculations, nonetheless, so there is much room for dialog.

Conceding that NDEs remain controversial, even with recent support from medical science, how do we interact with the universal non-local consciousness when we are living normally in the universe of the actual, if it does exist? In other words, exactly how is it possible our human bodies made up of quantum level particles that manifest in the physical world, access the presumed unitary consciousness at the quantum level?

It's all connected

Keeping in mind, if we are to accept the theory of the Big Bang[61], we are connected to the entire universe, quantum-entangled, to be more precise. To be clear, if the theory of the Big Bang is correct, everything that exists today was compressed into a single object that exploded to form the entire universe as we know it today. For this to be true, every single particle must have been entangled at the quantum level just to "fit" together. This level of fitness is beyond the human mind to comprehend.

Chaos to complex systems

All this said, somehow the chaos, the increasing entropy in the universe, found a way to organize and create life from inanimate components. Then found a way to evolve intelligent beings that have brains and the ability to contemplate their existence. This is a miracle greater than all the creation mythologies ever imagined by human beings and all the iconic descriptions in human folklore and religious mythology. And now we can study the functioning of our brains with a level of detail unimagined just 100 years ago.

Even with these explanations, the question remains how consciousness can continue after all brain functions cease? There are simply too many documented and verified cases of NDE's when all measurable brain functions have stopped.

Our language seems to have reached its limit in how to explain the unavoidable truths contained in UCE's and NDE's. The good news is we now know from this vantage point we can't see the entire truth about how we and the universe function together. When we admit we don't know, we are empowered to look deeper.

In summary, these theories suggest our bodies made up of quantum-entangled particles have the capacity to interact with quantum level phenomenon to produce the experience we call our minds. That somehow without any technological assistance, we, who are biological beings made up of quantum particles, can and do interact with what we have historically, mistakenly called the supernatural.

As speculated before, what we divide into the natural and supernatural are continuous phases of the same universe because the discovery of quantum mechanics provides a reasonable explanation for it to be so. People having NDE's are somehow able to experience the timelessness in the universe as it exists.

Another way of saying this is evolution has adapted us to fit the classical 3D level of reality. But we know by scientific investigation there is much more than we can perceive. Our religious mythologies have been trying to explain what we've always suspected beyond our ability to know. Now we may be starting to get a glimpse through the lenses of science.

Notes

Chapter 12

Language Reveals and Obscures Reality.

"The limits of my language mean the limits of my world."

Ludwig Wittgenstein

"The life of the mind cannot proceed without presuppositions," writes Dr. Bart Ehrman, New Testament scholar. As true as this is, it would be incomplete without also recognizing that these presuppositions are held in language, limited human language. And as the reader has already seen, German philosopher, Martin Heidegger said, "Language is a house of being."

There are whole books about this quote, so I won't attempt to add to that body of knowledge. Suffice to say that the idea contained in this quote serves as a point of departure for a deeper discussion on the limitations of language and what lies ahead in this chapter of the book.

Another way of understanding Wittgenstein's above quote is to say that language both reveals and obscures our experience of reality. At an even deeper level, it assists in the generation of our subjective experience, but that is the topic for another time. We live in this house called language, thinking that it contains all there is, blind to what we cannot perceive.

Historically, we created a new room of language to explain what we didn't understand, and that gave birth to religious mythology. Then about 600 BCE, Greek philosopher Thales of Miletus, a different kind of observer, described reality differently, and we began to create a new room of language called science.

Of course, religion and science are not the only rooms in this house. There are many, and as we progress in our knowledge of the cosmos, we build new rooms that expand our linguistic competence. But ultimately, we are bound within the walls of this house we call language. Even our most recent discoveries of deeper levels of reality, deeper than we could have imagined just 150 years ago, can only be understood within the context of the house of human language.

Then we developed writing and for about 6000 years recorded our history in various human languages giving birth to the great texts of our civilizations. But even with this vast body of knowledge we remain housed in the languages that are contained within.

Here is our dilemma: Language is self-referential, circular. Think of it this way. Each room in the house of language has at least two doorways. One that leads into its own room and another that always leads into another room. One can wander this house forever but never find a doorway that leads to anywhere but another room within the house. We are born, live and die in this house. If we're curious, we will explore other rooms, but too many of us stay in the room of our birth.

Many of us even get trapped in one room or another because we insist that this room is the one with all the answers. When we do, we not only ignore what we might find in the other rooms but also disregard the need to build new rooms to house new language. And yes, the best we can do is to build new rooms as additions to this house. We cannot build new free-standing houses. Some would argue that math is a different free-standing house, but it isn't. Without language, we couldn't understand math, so although it is another room, it is still of the same house.

The key point here is that no matter how clever one's argument is, for or against a point of view, everything we might say is limited within the House of Being we call language. So, when religious beliefs clash with scientific discoveries, they are limited by language and vice versa. Language limits all our arguments, beliefs, rationalizations, theories and counter-theories. And human language is insufficient for explaining what we are finding at the most fundamental level of the universe and in NDE's.

Does Consciousness Emerge from Our Brains?

Do we have brains, as distinct from the rest of our body? No. We have brains only because we make the distinction that this "three or four-pound" "segment or area" in our "heads," (all linguistic distinctions), is our brain. Just as we have objectively defined all the sub-components of our biology, none of them exist as independent segments of our bodies.

Imagine that you are peering into the opened torso of a human body and know nothing about it. What do you see? You see an undifferentiated mass of biological material until someone begins to point to specific areas and label them. But even then, you may only distinguish the heart, liver, lungs because they have been pointed out. But what of all the other parts that make up the mass? Unless you are taught the distinctions, you won't see vascular tissue, lymph glands, arteries, and veins, etc.

They are linguistic distinctions that allow us to understand our biology with the aid of labels. Where it not for those distinctions we are simply whole, undifferentiated, conscious living beings (also a linguistic distinction). We are also made of the same quantum properties that make up the rest of the universe. (again, all linguistic distinctions)

In this context, we are not separate from the universe, and our brain is not separate from the rest of our body. It is only differentiated because we distinguish it as such, another function of our egos. This fact allows us to think about the experience of consciousness coming from more than just that mass in our heads. (all linguistic distinctions)

So, as we progress in our discussion, keep in mind that we're using linguistic distinctions that only help us delineate and name the various areas and functions of our biology but don't truly describe raw reality. And by these distinctions, we have the assistance we need to understand how we function partially.

If you're still having trouble accepting this to be true, think about how the 2500-year-old Chinese, Japanese and Korean systems called Acupuncture[62] provide a completely different set of distinctions used to identify the various subsystems in the same human body described by Western medicine.

Remember, evolution has adapted us to fit our environment and not necessarily know the full and true nature of the universe. In this way, we are limited to language, or as Heidegger called it our House of Being. It is a way of describing, creating, and exploring ourselves and how we function. But the question is, how might we function that cannot be described by our limited linguistic abilities.

Let me count the ways. We are told by theoretical physicists that ordinary language cannot describe what exists beyond our ability to perceive at the classical 3D level where we are evolutionarily fit to function and live. We are told by NDEr's their experience is ineffable, beyond ordinary words to describe, and they use religious-cultural language to convey their stories. We are told by tradition religious stories about an afterlife that is clearly based on criteria communicated from NDEr's in the distant past.

In effect, trapped in Heidegger's *linguistic house of being* provides us enough linguistic capacity to describe that which we are evolutionarily fit to experience.

Linguistic Turn

Philosophers began the period called the Linguistic Turn in the early 20th century. During this period, they recognized the limitations of language in philosophical inquiry. A valued convention in philosophical inquiry is to be "presuppositionless." Hopefully by doing so, one can contribute innovative ideas that would move the discussion further into new territory.

They found that to be an impossibility. They had to acknowledge the limitations of language, which are all based on presuppositions. And presuppositions lock our thinking into a kind of circularity that defines the limits of any body of human knowledge, whether it be philosophy, religion, or science. (Rorty, 1992) They found that a great deal of what we think of as *reality* is really a convention of naming and characterizing; the convention which itself is called *language.*

Allow some poetic license here. There's a wonderful metaphor to describe our situation. We are standing in front of an infinitely large canvas. On it is a beautiful painting that is as wide and deep as the universe. It's so big we can't see the edges. But from our point of view, we can see an area of about 16 by 20 inches, and we think what we see is the whole painting. In fact, we insist it is the whole painting.

There is nothing so limiting to discovery as a sincere ignorance believed to be the result of rigorous investigation.

In summary, the many differences in theories about our reality that seem to conflict with all the other theories about reality are what Nietzsche referred to when he wrote "all things are subject to interpretation. Whichever interpretation prevails at a given time is a function of power, not the truth."

And this kind of power must be given. It cannot be taken. Usually, it's given to those we think deserve it if we are to accept their interpretation – that is if we're conscious of this fact. Unfortunately, many of us are not even aware that we've given over our authority to let someone else provide our interpretations. But hopefully some of us wake up and when we do, the decision is ours. Whose interpretations will you accept?

Think about that question before you answer. Because if this book serves its intended purpose, as you progress through the remaining chapters, you will be confronted with ideas that provoke serious questions about your previous interpretations of reality. And in considering them, you just may find another way of experiencing your life. Of course, this can't be forced, and ultimately, the decision is yours.

Notes

Chapter 13

Where Science and Religion Meet?

"Where a narrative of explanation might read something like *"the data led me to conclude...,"* a narrative of practice reads more like *"Huh, that's weird."*

Michael Shermer, Skeptic

Dr. Shermer, helps us define the issue very well. I don't think that was his intention, but his comment works to distinguish the difference between scientific evidence and subjective experience.

It's also interesting to note that much of the scientific denial of NDE's as an example of UCE's comes from the theoreticians and much of the evidence comes from those medical professionals, practitioners who see death every day in their clinics, hospitals, O.R.'s and E.D.'s. And yes, this is a subjective experience. But the whole illusion of objective evidence used by theoreticians to refute these findings based on subjective experience is, in fact, subjective itself. In the intellectual world today, it is difficult to find a serious proponent to argue for the existence of pure objectivity.

Although many modern religions are so contaminated with personal agendas and revisionist theories, it has not always been so. The common human subjective experience contained in all religious belief systems come together in a few general principles, which Shushan proposes originated from reports of NDE's, to begin with. These principles are reinforced when we study the aftereffects of NDEs: Love, compassion, empathy, and a willingness to help others. On this basis alone, religious believers should be open to further consideration of what follows.

If that's not enough, think about the possibility that St. Paul, the Apostle who planted the roots of the spiritual in the Christian Jewish sect that became Christianity might have had an NDE on the road to Damascus. In fact, as history shows us, St. Paul is the inventor of what we call Christianity today. Jesus knew nothing of it. He was born, lived and died an observant Jew.

In addition to the confirmation of subjective experience in religious principles, there is so much more. My readings, experience, limited knowledge of the great philosophical teachings of the world, and new discoveries in the cognitive sciences and theoretical physics—with special reference to the level of subatomic particle physics—have brought about the following speculations and questions. Some are shared by others; some are not. Remember, these are new doctrinal truths. Simply read what follows and let your imagination loose.

Because this book is a form of speculative non-fiction, there are notations separating scientifically proven facts from speculations and are indicated as such. This way the reader can have a more precise understanding of this chapter.

• **Fact**: We know we are not singular or individual beings. That impression is the function of our ego. It exists to allow us to operate in the reality of four-dimensional space-time but is not the basic structure of our existence. We are a quantum-entangled, interconnected part of the whole. In Einstein's words:

"A human being is part of the whole called by us the universe, a part limited in time and space. We experience ourselves, our thoughts, and feelings as something separate from the rest. A kind of optical delusion of consciousness. This delusion is a kind of prison for us, restricting us to our personal desires and to affection for a few persons nearest to us. Our task must be to free ourselves from the prison by widening our circle of compassion to embrace all living creatures and the whole of nature in its beauty. The true value of a human being is determined by the measure and the sense in which they have obtained liberation from the self. We shall require a substantially new manner of thinking if humanity is to survive." (Albert Einstein 1954)

We live in a non-local (interconnected) universe where everything and everyone is a unique spatial extension of an infinite web of probabilities.

Speculation: This universe of the actual emerges out of an infinite cosmic consciousness that permeates our entire bodies.

• From Chris Hedges, our concept of God is "our finite, flawed and imperfect expression of the infinite"; a humanized iconic symbol. **Speculation:** Although I do not believe in our iconic symbolism literally, I do believe *it* is everywhere and in everything. What we call, God, i.e., *It*, is the life force in the universe. *It* is what we experience as life itself. IT is what some refer to as a higher power. **Fact**: As Anita Moorjani[63] explained after her NDE in 2006, in her experience she learned that "God is a state of being."

Speculation: In this way, what we call "God's"[64] intention is manifest in the natural laws of the universe and us. This intention is manifest in our continuity and that of the universe. We could call it love in human terms. Stubborn clinging to revised religious beliefs and scientific ideologies keeps us from faith in the unknowable. Faith in the unknowable is faith in the natural functioning of the universe we may never fully understand; it is not a religious superstition. **Fact**: Everything and everyone emerges from a foam of probability that exists below the level of the quantum field. In Buddhist tradition, it is the source of the clear light that we become aware of at death. It is the origin of everything that exists.

• "Consciously living by love is the essence of life itself." (Long 2010) **Speculation**: We have popularized romantic love so much we limit our understanding to this context. Consequently, we do not fully comprehend it. It is so much more than human romantic love. Love is the ready and willing natural interaction of all processes in the actual fabric of our reality. It is the uninterrupted flow that falters when we introduce evil. Evil is not merely the opposite of good; it is a disruption in life's natural functioning. There is a deep and infinite intelligence embedded in the natural laws at the foundation of our universe, what physicists refer to as the Infinite Silence. What we call love are its logic and our essence. It is our natural way of being before the evolution of our personal egos. We can sometimes experience this level of reality through deep prayer and meditation.

• "Death is a metamorphosis of time – one more illusion born of our mental concepts." (Long 2010) **Speculation**: In other words, the awareness that comes from our limited biological capacity in this space-time and our finite concept of time here in the natural world occludes our view of other levels of the universe. **Fact**: Thousands of years of Eastern thought have come to the same conclusion. **Speculation**: It is a limited human perception that separates life and death into the actual of the physical universe and whatever lies beyond our direct experience.

When our bodies die, so does our gross consciousness and we will be relieved of our human biological limitations and can connect to the invisible, non-local, higher-dimensional space, proven to exist in the science of quantum mechanics and described in NDE's. This is the same higher-dimensional space we sometimes connect to in Unexplained Consciousness Events, UCE's. In other words, biological death and our egos lead to an awareness of our unbounded connection to and awareness of the deeper intelligence of the cosmos? The higher-dimensional form of clear light consciousness gives us access to the space-time continuum we cannot experience with our limited three-dimensional senses? **Fact**: Religions have been trying to describe this process as going to Heaven, Paradise, Valhalla, or Nirvana, etc. We are always connected to it. We can sometimes become of aware of it in deep meditation and prayer.

Fact: I repeat, theoretical physicist, Marcelo Gleiser explains our inability to see the true nature of reality this way: "If we could wear glasses with the prescription that the theory of relativity dictates, we would see the union of space and time in all its glory... Picturing space-time as a rubber sheet again, at the quantum level we would see oscillations that twist and contort it in myriad ways. Time runs amok. The consequences are mind-boggling. Without reliable measures of distance and time, or how to interpret them probabilistically, the whole edifice of physics crumbles. (M. Gleiser 2010)

Fact: We are 3D creatures evolved to fit this level of reality. Just as we are not able to perceive the electromagnetic fields and cosmic radiation that flows all around us, we are not evolved to fit in a universe of many dimensions. From here, our perspective is obscured. We can only speculate.

Speculation: Our personal consciousness continues and expands at bodily death so we can experience a higher dimensional space. **Fact**: Studies using so-called consciousness expanding psycho-active drugs have shown the exact opposite evidence of what was expected. The areas of the brain that supposedly would activate to produce these higher states show a reduction and not an increase in activity. "These studies on altered states of consciousness showed the exact opposite effects of what would support the theory of the brain as the creator of consciousness.

Dr. Eben Alexander, MD, Neuroscientist, "Speaking of Christof Koch: his interpretation of the 2012 study on psilocybin from Imperial College in London was identical to mine, as he wrote in Scientific American Mind (May 1, 2012). His subtitle was "To the great surprise of many, psilocybin, a potent psychedelic, reduces brain activity." Make no mistake: these repeated observations of a reduction in brain activity in major integrative centers in the most extraordinary psychedelic drug experiences are crucial pieces of evidence about the brain-mind relationship, and the fundamental nature of reality. The explanations will ultimately require a fundamental shift in the assumptions built deeply into our scientific world view—assumptions based on pure physicalism, that the only stuff in the universe is physical stuff, and that the brain creates consciousness."[65]

Fact: We have always been and are still united with everything in the universe. We are not separate and individual. Are we temporal-spatial extensions (single lives) of the continuous universe? In other words, specific expressions of infinite probability reified as one life span. **Speculation**: Consciousness has always been here and always will be? We are all connected to it in this life and only sometimes aware of it under unusual circumstances or deep meditation and prayer.

• **Fact**: Our concept of time in the physical world is one of finitude. There is no time in the quantum landscape; "it represents only a mapping of potential universes." (Gleiser 2010) There is only pure probability. Time begins when we reduce the probability to the actual. Another way of saying this is a quote from Roger Penrose I've used before: "we move from the time of the *actual* universe, which is zero to the speed of light, to the time of the "probable" universe, which is from the speed of light to infinity." At infinity, there is no time. The sequential experience of time is an illusion created by our limited view, which comes with our three-dimensional limitations.

• **Fact**: All living creatures are needed as an integral part of the universe unfolding. The universe is in the constant process of creating itself. **Speculation**: It will never be complete because the quantum is infinite. We each contribute to that continual creation. This may be the purpose of our lives. Our lives may provide the objective reduction that brings forth the *actual living* universe from the inanimate *poised realm* of probability. In this way, our individual lives and that of every other living creature are each co-creating an important part of the actual universe. The living universe! This may allow for the existence of other life forms in this and on other worlds, all participating in the co-creation of life.

• **Speculation**: Isn't every sentient being of critical importance as they observe and create their portion of the living universe of the actual? In other words, consciousness is not limited to human beings and is ubiquitous throughout all the levels of sentient life forms. The lowliest life form is conscious of a portion of reality of which the highest form is completely unaware and vice versa. They are all needed to create the chain of existence that began billions of years ago.

• **Speculation**: Moral evil exists in the world, not because a loving God allows it. **Fact**: It requires the action of a person to bring it into the physical world. It only happens in the manifest world, which is the classical level of the universe.

Reality simply <u>is</u>; it is neutral. We bring the meaning to it by our actions and intentions. **Fact**: If we want to be rid of evil in the actual world, we must do it ourselves by living with love. We cannot blame an iconic God for the evil humans do. The god created by man does not change the actual. We do it by our actions. Why? We have free will. We have the freedom to actualize any potential—to make manifest in the actual, everything that is probable in the quantum.

• **Speculation**: Natural disasters, illnesses, untimely deaths, and all those events that cause suffering—even to the innocent—are not evil.

They are the result of the normal functioning of our natural laws. The actual universe is indifferent to the suffering caused by natural disasters. Its laws function as they do regardless of the effects on us. Its intention is to actualize itself through us, by us living our lives bringing the probable into the actual. When the innocents suffer from natural disasters, it is not evil. It is a natural phenomenon at the manifest level of the universe. There is nothing to blame on a putative intentional agent that might cause or prevent it.

We have prayer and faith to help us survive these events. Prayer is an action that provides the strength to get through our difficulties. When prayer has an effect, it comes from influencing the reduction of the probable into the actual and not from a supernatural being. Faith is a way of knowing these events are a natural functioning of an unfolding universe; knowing everything will eventually be okay.

• **Speculation**: There is no reward or punishment meted out by a punitive God as a judge. There is only karma. Karma is the primary mechanism for our spiritual evolution. Our task is continual learning and improvement through experiencing the effects of our actions. In this context, judgment makes no sense. Judgment is a human attribute. There is no judgment, per se, in the universe. There is only cause and effect. The way we live our lives causes the effects we produce. Good is its own reward. Evil is its own punishment.

• **Speculation**: There is no eternity in human terms. Eternity depends on our earthly concept of time. Our human concept of eternity erroneously presumes a physical nature to an afterlife because all living beings have a beginning and an end. The concept of spiritual beings shaped liked human forms then being resurrected on the judgment day is unique to monotheistic religions.

What we call eternity is *sempiternity*, which is the existence of a temporal body forever. After our consciousness moves to the next stage, we are no longer physical beings. We are no longer temporal beings. In this dimension, there is only the now. It is not eternity. We cannot fully comprehend the experience of "only the present," so we mistakenly call it eternity.

No one burns in the fires of hell, and no one sits on the clouds of heaven. What we call heaven might be the experience of having access to all the knowledge in the universe, —becoming an unbounded and unified observer. In other words, being connected to the *sublime and limitless*: the total Truth. Some of our religions call this the experience of knowing God in heaven. Our goal is to know and be in concert with the wisdom of the universe.

Fact: In some way or another, all religions have postulated the above beliefs but have placed human metaphors and, consequently, human reasoning for the actions needed to achieve them.

This whole chapter makes more sense if we think of ourselves not as distinct objects but as spatial extensions. Once again, an ocean wave is a spatial extension of the ocean. Although the wave appears as a distinct object, it is always still the ocean in substance. It doesn't disappear entirely when it reaches the shore and dissipates. It simply returns to its original state as the ocean. We are never separate from the basic fabric of the universe. We are always in it, from it and a part of it; a temporary spatial extension of it.

In summary, many qualified professionals, believe certain NDEs are authentic. If so, consciousness is doing something we simply do not understand. So, these veridical portions of NDE's are Unexplained Consciousness Experiences.

Some scientists too?

In his book, *The Fabric of the Cosmos*, Brian Greene, describes the meaning of spacetime.[66] He uses the metaphor of the frozen river of spacetime, where all events, everywhere and everywhen are whole and complete. Consistent with Einstein's theories, each of us has a relative view that creates what Greene calls "now slices" or individual views from each of our present moments. "Undeniably, our conscious experience seems to sweep through the [now] slices. It is as though our minds provide the projector light referred to earlier so that moments of time come to life when the power of consciousness illuminates them." (Greene, The Hidden Reality 2011)

With these scientific facts serving as a foundation, my questions are: If everything, everywhere, and *everywhen* exists in a space-time loaf as we know it does; if each of our *now slices* constitutes that space-time loaf as we know they do; if our individual consciousness illuminates our now slices as we know it does; if events can be experienced by different observers in time before or after they occur, then in order for that space-time loaf to maintain its integrity, our consciousness must somehow continue.

So, the question is if the consciousness that illuminates our now slices disappeared when we die biologically, how could the space-time loaf exist? If it continues, would not our instances of now continue to exist somewhere, somehow? Another way of asking is, how could the space-time loaf still exist when our personal consciousness that illuminates our now slices, that make it up, disappear with our demise? In this way, consciousness would seem like a non-reductive primitive element of the universe. It is as necessary as matter and energy, or the space-time loaf couldn't exist as we know it does.

Einstein said, "The further the spiritual evolution of mankind advances, the more certain it seems to me that the path to genuine religiosity does not lie through the fear of life, and the fear of death, and blind faith, but through striving after rational knowledge."[67]

The universe is unfolding as it should. In this regard, we and nature are not flawed. We are not always virtuous, loving, or lovable. We are always an integral part of the cosmos. We are the way the cosmos knows itself. We are conscious!

Notes

Part Two

True or False

"I would not die for my beliefs because I might be wrong."

Bertrand Russell

If you are reading this section, you are not convinced that NDE's as a subset of UCE's are authentic. Chances are your resistance to the previous chapters fall into the domains of religion, science or both.

I make this assumption based on my experience. My resistance falls into both of those domains of presuppositions. Remember Ehrman's words, "The life of the mind cannot proceed without presuppositions."

Even so, you've found the previous section compelling enough to read more. And you are open to challenging your thinking.

Congratulations, you are among the rarest of readers; critical thinkers who can hold two opposing thoughts in mind without needing to discount one or the other. In this section, you will have lots of opportunities to enjoy that experience.

The section you just completed offers a different explanation of the reality we all take for granted. If you are like me, you had to overcome the noise in your head. The noise I refer to is the ongoing narrative that accompanies every waking moment of our lives.

Hopefully, by now you understand that the narrative being voiced is made up of presuppositions about everything you experience. And those presuppositions are there to protect you from harm.

At first glance, that seems good. And to some extent it is. But here's the problem. That narrative voice doesn't discriminate. It is simply reactive, not only to external events but also to its own continuous monologue.

Given its proclivity to react to itself, this monologue can keep us thinking in closed recursive loops. The result is often the end of new experience and consequently new learning.

Unless confronted, you can fall into a mood of depression and despondency. Every day will feel like every other day, and the world will continue to disappoint you. Why wouldn't it? Your monologue is using all your past experiences to warn against the dangers of new experiences.

So, what can we do? The first step is to realize that your monologue is not you. It is a traveling companion who lives in your head. An idiot who never shuts up and is always ready to advise you with any number of ridiculous responses that very often have nothing to do with your present experience.

When you realize this, you begin to awake and can get ready to learn from the life you're living right now. Until then, that idiot in your head can obscure anything of present value with fears, worries, threats, and dangers from your past.

This new awareness, this new wakefulness, can be the difference between living each year of your life anew or the same year repeatedly until you die of boredom or exhaustion.

The following chapters will attack many of the cognitive devices we use to justify continuing to listen to the monologue offered by the idiots in our heads. Odds are before you finish the chapters that remain, you'll have many opportunities to confront them. Confront them with new ideas or let them win. The choice is yours.

If you leave this book with nothing else, remember you are not the monologue. You are the one listening to it.

Chapter 14

Confronting Religious Beliefs

"According to science, the universe began as a swirl of gas that, as it cooled, spun off the Ten Commandments."

Robert Brault

"Virtually everything in our immediate physical environment is made up of quanta that have been interacting with other quanta in this manner from the big bang to the present.... Also, consider ... that quantum entanglement grows exponentially with the number of particles involved in the original quantum state and that there is no theoretical limit on the number of these entangled particles. If this is the case, the universe on a very basic level could be a vast web of particles, which remain in contact with one another over any distance in "no time" in the absence of the transfer of energy or information. This suggests, however, strange or bizarre it might seem, that all of physical reality is a single quantum system that responds together to further interactions." (Radin, 2009)

As we can see in the preceding description, our whole concept of a universe of discrete objects separated by space must change. Picture the universe as an infinitely large coherent fabric of intermingled probability waves of particles able to collapse into actual by some mechanisms we do not yet fully understand. In it, everything that exists connects to everything else. There is nothing that is not connected to everything else. At this level, there is no time and communications between and among the points in this fabric are instant.

Knowing this is now scientific fact, the religious cosmology of the dual realities of heaven and earth, the epistemology of an inerrant biblical text, the ontology of a dual nature in body and soul, all call for a serious re-examination.

Monotheistic religions settled the great human questions over 3000 years ago, with the development of a religious mythology; a mythology that pointed to but wasn't fully able to explain the truths contained therein.

The point is that although religious mythology may not be literally true, it represents monumental accomplishments in the revelations of certain attributes of the universe that in preliterate times could only be explained and understood in human stories.

In the oldest religious belief systems, other worlds exist; natural and supernatural. We live this life in the natural world and strive to qualify our souls for admittance into heaven, paradise, or some other world in the afterlife. This, of course, depends on the ontology of dualism—we are body and soul. Science, on the other hand, kept finding evidence supporting the belief we are simply biological beings, which led to the conclusion we are only physical beings, and this is it.

This ongoing conflict in belief systems goes to the core issue of the philosophical dispute, which is the essence of this book. Consequently, this situation leaves no room for discussion if we remain at opposite poles. On the other hand, the middle ground might provide unusual answers and give us much more peace, let alone a clearer picture of this mysterious cosmos. But we will need openness to new ways of understanding what it is to be a human being, what constitutes valid knowledge, and how we understand the nature of the cosmos.

In our current religious context, it is easy to be skeptical about the findings in NDE studies. They don't precisely fit within any religious belief system. While it is true that those NDEr's who are religious before their experience will often use iconic religious figures in their reports, their religious stories about these figures don't match up perfectly to faith traditions.

This is ironic because we have good evidence that shows the original religions were influenced by NDE's.

Reconciliation

Religious faith is based on certain doctrines that have evolved over thousands of years of history. Most of the fundamental principles in these doctrines do not require evidence. Consequently, opinions based on such principles are erroneously offered as assertions. Even though these erroneous assertions do not have the requisite evidence to support them, fervent believers are often willing to die in their defense.

It's a waste of time to try to reconcile the many different interpretations of Christianity—one of many religions. There seem to be as many interpretations as there are people. The conflicts arise because religious belief is justified by faith, and faith requires no evidence.

Is there any objective way to test the validity of religious beliefs? Probably, objective analysis will never explain the variability of subjective experience. So, to examine religious belief at the level of the individual will yield even more variation.

The Point Being?

There is a central distinction here. We're not arguing against faith per se. But when considering it, at least two forms of faith are important to consider: (1) Religious faith in one's beliefs. (2) Personal faith in the unknowable. Religious faith in beliefs usually stops further searching. Personal faith in the unknowable opens the door to discovery.

The big challenge to religious believers is to recognize and acknowledge the need to question faith in their beliefs. This is a big obstacle for those among them who insist they have the only correct theology. Convinced of this, why would anyone consider new information?

Well, I think there are two possible answers: They believe they know God's true word and if you have God's true word, why would you consider another view? Or the idea of having faith in the unknowable is simply too difficult to imagine.

This is the trial every individual must be willing to face when their faith is shaken by some tragic event that makes no sense in the context of their beliefs. This is sometimes called a crisis of faith.

How to Proceed?

On a general basis, if religious believers are interested in evaluating what we find in authentic UCE's, they will need to examine the religious errors, or misjudgments, based on three philosophical positions mentioned at the beginning: (1) the ontology of flawed and separate humans, (2) the cosmology of a dual and separate universe—natural and supernatural realms, and (3) the rejection of factual analysis in favor of blind faith in clearly unsubstantiated beliefs.

As an example, consider the many times major religious teachings have changed over the centuries. As modern technological and scientific progress continues, some religious organizations have the integrity to adjust their teachings to comply with new discoveries. Some see these changes as heresy and remain unconvinced that their beliefs are obsolete. And a blind faith in this kind of belief requires a refusal to acknowledge the limitations of the source of the knowledge they consider valid. In this way, there can never be a reconciliation.

Here's the good news: Science is telling us and religion can abide by this without losing its core values: Our nature and that of the cosmos is of one unified whole. It is a universe with so many levels we cannot perceive them.

Our inventions of science and religion should work toward human progress in this life. To merge them both into a more holistic understanding would require believers to reinterpret their beliefs to include modern understandings of the nature of reality and who we are in the process of co-creating it. Believers can continue to be concerned with living a virtuous life but for even more accurate reasons.

By raising these points, we're not questioning the value of living a virtuous life. But belief in an afterlife is not the only reason for wanting to live such a life. What we're calling into question is the usual justification taught in religious doctrine. This justification is based on an incomplete and, therefore, erroneous explanation of the essence of our cosmos. It is based on the way we experience it at the "3D" *classical, every day,* level of reality.

Today, we know the way we humans experience the universe is not the way it is. Thousands of years ago, they did not. They trusted common sense experience of reality and this reality had too many mysteries to be explained by people with severely limited scientific competence. In this way, our religious beliefs are based on precarious foundations; the human experience of a universe that functions in immensely different ways than they could even imagine, let alone understand.

While ancient reports of NDE's caused them to know that there was more than they could perceive, the religious mythology that emerged contained their assessments but not literal truths. Down through the ensuing centuries, we have turned these myths into concrete beliefs and created religious institutions to have authority over those who believe them. When we put authority structures in religious belief systems, we gave birth to dogmas. These dogmas have firmed up into ideologies. Until we can confront them with our new discoveries, they will continue to be primary barriers to new learning.

In summary, we are now in a new age of discovery. We are beginning to recognize and appreciate the mysterious nature of our universe. Religion can be an ally or an enemy of new learning. If it remains in its historical adversarial position, it will suffer a long and protracted death spiral toward irrelevance; its current place in many modern countries. This would be a great loss to humanity. Science cannot explain everything. We are so much more than assemblages of biological components.

We live in a universe of mystical proportions. At the deepest levels, we sense its mysteries far exceed our ability to comprehend. Religion allows us to contemplate these mysteries but cannot provide literal descriptions. We must settle for the mythos, the mystical, instead of the logos, the rational. The attempt to explain the mythos rationally leads to idolatry.

From John Caputo's book, What Would Jesus Deconstruct, "Meister Eckhart, said God is unnameable and therefore omni nameable, and so He prays, I pray God to rid me of God. I pray (the unnameable) God to rid me of (the idol I have named) God."

He elaborates, "Orthodoxy is idolatry if it means holding "correct opinions about God" – "fundamentalism" is the most extreme and salient example of such idolatry, but not if it means holding faith in the right way, that is, not holding it at all but being held by God, in love and service."

Before you object to the term, "by God, in love and service," and dismiss this whole piece because you don't believe God exists, please remember, the term God here, is a placeholder for that core mystery that seems to permeate this amazing cosmos.

Notes

Chapter 15

Changes Needed in Scientific Beliefs

"For the scientist who has lived by his faith in reason, the story ends like a bad dream. He has scaled the mountains of ignorance; he is about to conquer the highest peak; as he pulls himself over the final rock, he is greeted by a band of theologians who have been sitting there for centuries."[68]

Robert Jastrow, American astronomer, physicist, and cosmologist

As I've pointed out throughout this book, one of the limitations is our neurophysiological make-up, the same make-up that is very limited as a way of experiencing the true nature of the universe. We are *creatures of the middle world.* We cannot directly experience the infinitesimal level of subatomic particles or the vast and seemingly boundless universe with billions of galaxies and a trillion billion stars. Our whole logic goes askew when we try to explain what we find at the quantum level. Our words will not suffice when we try to describe the whole functioning of the universe by our limited experience at the classical level of reality. We are still unable to explain how the results of scientific observations are created by our conscious interactions.

One of the interesting findings in NDE's is that people's reports contain descriptions of reality exactly like those given to us by theoretical physicists. Yes, they do use their own cultural and religious references in their descriptions. In most instances, they tell us that the experience they had is difficult if not impossible to explain with common language.

So, my purpose in this chapter is to convince the reader to reconsider our capacity to accurately describe how the universe functions in any terms, especially commonly understood Newtonian/ Einsteinian models. And in doing so, see how our common-sense experience of reality is minimal and inadequate. Hopefully, we will loosen our grasp on what we consider our understanding of the reality we inhabit. Until we do, new learning will be difficult.

To illustrate how our common-sense views do not represent reality, these are some of the critical, scientific revelations. Our difficulty in explaining them is partially caused by our inability to perceive them directly. It's also because we cling to a logic that prohibits their very existence in our mechanistic model of reality.

Consider how counter-intuitive they seem to our common sense. It is not necessary to have a deep scientific understanding of these examples, but rather to simply reflect on the wonder of their complexity and how they differ from the way we think about our reality. By doing so, it becomes obvious that a whole new ontology begs for recognition.

If you are still skeptical, you are not alone, remember Einstein's uncertainty about his own equations. None the less, he was one of the greatest contributors to our knowledge of the cosmos.

Einstein's Special Theory of Relativity proved the speed of light is the ultimate velocity *within* the universe. We now know at the quantum level, speed is not limited by the same formulae. There is no time there.

We also know the universe is expanding at a rate faster than the speed of light at the farthest edges. The speed of the expansion of space does not violate the maximum speed *within* it. Consequently, we will never see the light coming from the far regions of the universe. Because of this, how can we ever know the true size or age of the universe? That is if it has a size and age. (Reminder: size and age are human linguistic constructions).

When measured, the speed of light is uniform regardless of how fast the observer is traveling. One can be traveling toward or away from it and it does not change its speed relative to the individual. This finding is counter-intuitive based on our common sense understanding of relative speed in our everyday experience.

For instance, if a person was on a train at night traveling seventy miles per hour and could see the light from another train moving toward her on another track at sixty miles per hour, she could say the trains are closing the gap at a speed of one hundred and thirty miles per hour. This would be true for any observer on the train or standing aside.

Not true with light. Regardless of the speed of the trains to the observer, light is always traveling at a constant velocity. The relative speed of an observer does not get added to or subtracted from the speed of light.

We live in a universe, which seems to us middle creatures as though objects are separate from each other by space. This is what physicists call a *local* universe. It means cause and effect only work on objects coming into direct contact, for instance, a bat hitting a baseball.

We now know the universe is *non-local*. Objects can be *quantum-entangled*, regardless of how far apart they are. An action in one location can have an immediate effect on an entangled object on the other side of the universe, faster than the speed of light, the ultimate velocity at the classical level.

Metaphorically, it would be like swinging a bat here and the ball instantly reacting in another galaxy. The universe of discrete objects that we experience emerges from a coherent non-local whole we don't experience. At that level, the human concepts of time and speed have no meaning.

Our universe seems to function according to two sets of laws. One set at the classical level (where we 3D creatures are) and another set at the subatomic level beyond our perceptual range.

Physicists are still divided on the search for a grand unifying theory to unite and explain both. Some believe we will never find it, even if it does exist. For those, who believe in a grand unifying theory, the most promising theory of everything is *supersymmetry*, which until recently, seemed to confirm the popular Standard Model of Particle Physics.

The SMPP is "a theory concerning the electromagnetic, weak, and strong nuclear interactions, as well as classifying all the subatomic particles known. It was developed throughout the latter half of the 20th century, as a collaborative effort of scientists around the world.

"The current formulation was finalized in the mid-1970s upon experimental confirmation of the existence of quarks. More recently, the search for proof of the existence of the Higgs boson has caused concern about the accuracy of the Standard Model. Up until now its success in explaining a wide variety of experimental results, the Standard Model has been regarded as the "theory of *almost* everything."[69]

But as usual, each discovery seems to create more questions. The evidence for the Higgs boson shows it has a weight of 125 GeV (gigaelectronvolts). This finding leaves the question of its stability open.

In other words, its GeV is between two points (115 and 145) and that could indicate different models for explaining the universe. We still don't know which model is the most accurate. The first of 115 would indicate that the SMPP is on track to explain the basic nature of the universe. The second at 145 would give more weight to the theory of a multiverse, where ours is just one of an infinite number of universes.

The key difference is that in a multiverse there would be no standard model of anything. No coherent explanation for our existence other than the chance happening that the nature of this universe supports life.

Time does not flow, we do. Physicists visualize the universe as a *space-time loaf* we pass through as we live our lives. Each of us experiences a series of *now slices*, and because our consciousness and memory organize them sequentially, we experience time as *flowing* in one direction. Time is sequential to us, but not the universe. Time is also relative to the individual. Each of us has a different experience of time. In scientific fact, as an object moves, time slows down for that object. The difference is so minute that we don't experience it at our level of the universe.

But it is a sufficient difference to make automatic adjustments to our GPS satellites, or they would eventually send us erroneous signals because time passes slower for them than us here on the surface of the earth.

We cannot scientifically explain how our mind interacts with matter. We are beginning to suspect a level of reality between the actual and the probable called: *the poised*. Remember Dr. Stuart Kauffman[70] proposes our minds can *decohere* and *re-cohere* quantum behavior repeatedly in this realm.

Think of it this way. This is only an analogy and not intended to be scientifically accurate. A thought held in our minds can come (decohere) and go (recohere) back into the quantum wholeness. Once we act on that thought, we have reduced it to the physical reality we experience. (Decohere it from the quantum wholeness). We've taken it from the probability into the actual.

Our brains are quantum-embedded systems as, Roger Penrose, an English mathematical physicist; and others suggest. This being so, we are connected to the universal non-local consciousness in a dimension we are not equipped to experience by the same mechanism. Or as Professor Donald Hoffman suggests, we only have brains because we create them by distinguishing that area of our biological body as a separate component. We are not discrete objects but spatial-temporal extensions of the universe itself.

These and other scientific findings make our common-sense experience of the universe obviously incomplete. Physiologically, we cannot experience the virtually infinite information flowing in, through and around us. We live in a universe of seemingly infinite activity. Our neurophysiology has evolved to be a consciousness filter, which allows us to perceive what we must to survive and protect us from sensory stimulus flooding. If we could sense all that is happening around us, we would be overwhelmed. We sense only what is necessary; only that which fits us to our evolutionary niche. The rest goes unnoticed in our *common-sense* experience.

Think of this point this way; we know by observation that certain other life forms on our planet can navigate long distances without the aid of the devices we use to do the same. For instance, geese, hummingbirds, Monarch butterflies. These creatures have adapted an ability to observe and use completely different features of the reality we share. Yes, we can figure out these seeming mysteries. Yes, we can develop tools to help us perceive the same realities. But other sentient beings have the natural evolutionarily developed capacities because they can perceive a level of reality that evades us naturally. In simple terms, these animals don't need maps or a GPS to get where they're going.

Even the flow of information we can sense is reduced by the processing capacity of our neurophysiology. For instance, dealing with our visual input, our retina is exposed to ten million bits of information per second. By the time this data gets to our visual cortex, only one hundred to one hundred and ten bits per second can be processed. This infinitesimal portion of information is the basis of our assessments (our models or cognitive maps) of how the world works. We simply process too little to take firm positions on the true nature of all reality.

Add to this, the fact a tiny stream of processed information cannot account for what we call consciousness. Remember, consciousness depends on memory to function, cognitive scientists call it intrinsic activity. In this way, we are always projecting what we already believe onto the world around us. Contrary to the logic of our common sense, we see what we already believe, not believe what we see in present time.

Now, consider that all thinking is infused with emotion, and we have some strong feelings about what we believe. We come to what psychologists call: *confirmation* and *disconfirmation* bias. We distort even the minimal information input we receive and confirm facts supporting our existing point-of-view and disconfirm those which do not.

There is no human effort more powerful than confirmation bias to justify our existing point of view. If we cling to what we already believe, we will make little progress in understanding our full nature and the nature of the universe we inhabit.

Having said all this, we see the beginning of a new age of discovery, which will again merge philosophical and scientific inquiry. However, for this to be effective, the old beliefs must yield, and we need to build a new way of thinking about our common human questions.

In summary, the scientific methods which help us discover more about how our universe functions are based on a mechanistic ontology re-enforced by an Einsteinian epistemology. There is a paradox here. The very methods that help us learn more prohibit learning more. Our new discoveries are always judged by the previous models. And this makes sense. It keeps our learning grounded in mutually agreed scientific pragmatism. The peer review process works to screen the wheat from the chafe, but there have been points in history when that same process kept us in the dark. E.g., the Church's authority to determine what would become public knowledge based on their dogmas.

NDE's and consciousness studies are giving us clues to a new way of understanding levels of the universe that religions have been pointing to for thousands of years. If we insist that scientific orthodoxy is the only valid route to new knowledge we just might miss the most important good news about human possibilities.

Notes

Chapter 16

The Illusion of Certainty

> "The only certainty is that nothing is certain."
>
> Pliny The Elder[71]

Certainty or Certitude?

People who've had authentic NDE's are sure of their experience. Their own subjective experience is the source of the knowledge they use as evidence for their argument. People who deny them are also sure they are a hoax. Their source of knowledge is usually based on the scientific method and its ability to disqualify anything that can't be intersubjectively verified, often called objective evidence. Who's right and who's wrong? Let's look at the question of certainty before we try to decide.

Einstein himself resisted his own formulae that told him the universe is expanding. Not once but twice. The first time he was so certain, that he added what became known as the *cosmological constant*. In layperson's terms, it was a fudge factor that allowed him to justify his error of interpretation in his calculations. Moreover, the second time he met with Georges Lemaitre[72] and dismissed Lemaitre's formulae that proved the expansion theory of the universe. He reviewed Lemaitre's work and dismissed it out of hand. He was *certain* of his own conclusions; a mistake he admitted haunted him the rest of his life.

As Einstein demonstrated, certainty implies a thorough consideration of evidence and eliminates any shadow of a doubt. Many of us are sure of our beliefs as was Einstein. So, what we consider certainty is our *certitude*. Certitude is personal and can be based more on one's beliefs rather than verifiable facts. It is not the test of certainty. If we test our certitude to its logical conclusion, many times we end in the state of aporia—that state of confusion discussed in French philosopher Jacques Derrida's[73] theory of deconstruction.

Most of us do not consider questioning, let alone testing, our certitude to its logical conclusion. This is very apparent in popular culture today. For instance, we have many committed people on both sides of the war between religious fundamentalism and modern secularism. This socio-religious polarity is not only in our national discourse but is destroying whole nations in other parts of the world. These people rest on their certitude—each believing his or her "facts" are correct; each finding validation in different epistemological sources.

When we look closer, we find the same level of personal certitude in contradictory beliefs. This should be our first clue that the logic leading to our certitude is questionable. Nevertheless, personal certitude does not change easily. We all seem to have a rigid wall of emotions surrounding our beliefs. They give us the assurance we need to validate our point of view. The acceptance of new information usually involves a loss of the old. No one enjoys the pain of loss. So, resistance to changing our beliefs is a natural *pain avoidance* response.

"Assurance is a feeling of confidence resulting from our subjective experience. It is self-referential. We can't base it on certainty because there is no such thing as absolute certainty, although there is enough to provide the assurances sufficient for living our lives."[74]

So, we are living our lives, assured by our personal stories, which emerge from the *preferred* stories of our popular cultures of origin. And as we know, various cultures consider themselves certain of so many opposite positions that it makes international politics one of the most complex areas of human interactions.

We prefer our stories, both personal and cultural because we trust their coherency, but they cannot provide certainty. This means that in the place of certainty, certitude arises from the illusory elimination of doubt. Moreover, when it does, it usually inhibits new learning and discovery.

The Closed Loop of Certainty

Our stories are closed recursive loops, and they do provide the assurances we need. The clear majority of Americans, well over seventy percent, look to religious stories for assurance during uncertain times. These stories contain religious beliefs. Many people base their certitude on them. The ostensible but imagined coherency and the long history of religion add to their credibility and gives them comfort. In other words, we trust them without question because they have been around for a long time. Consequently, we will make whatever revisions we need to maintain their coherence. In this way, we can remain assured and ultimately comfortable. To these people, the reports from most NDEer's do not fit their stories of what happens after death.

Of course, there are others who disregard religious beliefs and look to science to find the assurances they need. To be sure, their experiences are also compiled or arranged into coherent stories to provide comfort. To them, an NDE might just be the last physiological responses of a dying brain.

The coherency of our stories helps to diminish doubt and alleviate anxiety by reinforcing personal certitude, but it will not assure certainty. Certainty cannot be found in either religion or science, even though as I've claimed throughout this book, the Newtonian mechanistic model says this universe is deterministic.

Now we know it is not. Nevertheless, we are driven throughout our lives to find *certain truths* so we can rest assured. We seek it in our stories, even if we must change a few details to keep them intact because above all other factors, our stories must remain coherent. Accuracy does not matter—all that matters is they explain life in terms which do not conflict with what we already believe. This forms a powerful resistance to societal change.

Our Stories Give Us Assurance Beyond the Grave.

It goes even further than the end of our life; religious stories are so important to us we extend them beyond death.

Even now with the study of Near Death Experiences, what may or may not happen to us after death has been a matter of faith, not evidence and, therefore, could not exist in the realm of certainty. However, new doorways to discovery are opening in this regard.

Even Math Fails.

No one has yet crossed the gap between the end of mathematical calculations and a complete theory to explain our universe. Even classical math, the most certain of all humankind's developments, fails at the most basic level of our existence, the quantum.

With the discovery of the quantum level, we know the essential quality of the fundamental basis of the universe is uncertainty. Since the development of chaos theory, we are aware even systems described mathematically are capable of chaotic reorganization. This makes outcomes unpredictable at our classical level of reality. A simple illustration is our difficulty in accurately predicting the weather beyond a day or two.

Theoretical biologist and complex systems researcher, Stuart Kauffman, offers this advice: "... we cannot follow Newton's prescription: specify the initial conditions; specify the boundary conditions; specify the laws of motion and integrate to derive the entailed future trajectory of the system. We cannot do this because we do not know ahead of time the boundary conditions. This suffices to show that there is no *entailing law* for the evolution of the biosphere." (Italics added)[75]

In addition to our inability to predict future initial conditions, even if we could, they can be imperceptibly different from our mathematical calculations. This all amounts to our failure to predict outcomes with certainty even from systems fully described by mathematical equations.

In effect, in our universe, chaos and order seem deeply linked. Every future event remains probable, yet impossible to predict with certainty. In all instances, when human beings claim certainty, we only have personal certitude to give us the assurances we need. The existential reality is we are certainty-seeking creatures in an indeterminate universe.

At the classical 3D level, there appears an objective material foundation, governed by natural laws, partially perceived by us and metaphorically described in our stories. We know now that our evolutionarily adapted perception does not reveal the truth about the totality of the substance of that reality. What we observe is a creation of our method of observation.

At the quantum level, there exists only the probability of such a material reality. There seems to be an undefined line between the macro and microscopic levels of reality that no one has yet identified. However, we have proven the universe functions according to different laws at each level and have yet to find the unifying principle if one does exist.

Our Stories Are Just Stories.

To cope, we have created stories that attempt to explain the unexplainable. If we can see them as just stories—relevant, useful, ubiquitous, but not certain—we will realize the only creative human option is to learn to live with our questions. No matter what new story we create to believe, it does not contain all the answers; it simply cannot provide certainty.

This leaves us with the only realistic choice: Open ourselves to simple faith in the unknowable. When we do this, we can continually question our stories and interpretations of the events in our lives. We can dwell in expectant inquiry and continually search for the elusive truth. It is the only honest position to take in an uncertain universe like ours. Moreover, the only position to take when we consider the experiences of NDE's that meet all the well-established criteria for authenticity.

We are more available to this if we openly recognize and accept that our answers contradict themselves. All that said, most of us will continue to depend on our old stories because they give us a sense of that important and elusive certainty, simply not attainable. In other words, our resistance to questioning beliefs can rob us of the experience of real discovery by giving us a false sense of certainty.

World War III is already underway. It is between Religious Fundamentalism and Cultural Secularism. It is a battle between the Absolutism[76] of Fundamentalism, a theory where values such as truth or morality are absolute and unconditional, and the Relativism[77] of Secularism, a theory that right and wrong are not absolute,

With all this uncertainty, the only haven seems to be an openness to the possibilities that abound in this amazing universe. An uncertainty that says there are mysteries we will never understand completely, but we can and will get glimpses. Moreover, the world will not collapse if we change our minds when we see the evidence that disconfirms our beliefs. There are good reasons to adhere to our principles but still be open to new discoveries. There are no complete and total answers. If we are to live in the questions, we need this form of simple curiosity.

When we live exclusively in a limited model of reality and are then exposed to another, blind faith in this model should die naturally if we are to make progress. It usually doesn't. The world's cultural complexity is now being broadcast by mass, unfiltered, global communications which make our challenge more difficult. This enhances our awareness and exacerbates our concerns, but it should also accelerate questions if change is to occur.

Instead, the fear of loss that comes with the growing irrelevance of naïve realism [78] is driving some people to even more convoluted stories. They are bending their beliefs out of shape so much they are barely grounded in any reality any longer.

Modern politics and contemporary fundamentalist religion are distinct, fertile areas to study this phenomenon. What's not so obvious are the limitations we place our new discoveries by believing in the certainty of religious and scientific ideologies.

There is more to be gained for all of humanity than just the acceptance of unusual experiences like UCE's if we can allow ourselves to question these ideologies.

In summary, to grow in wisdom, we need to recognize the futility in our search for certainty. When we do, we can become different observers and open whole new areas of investigation. The circumstances will not change, but if we become new observers, we will see them as though with new eyes.

When we become new observers by questioning our beliefs, we might begin to learn real, simple faith in the unknowable. When we do, we come full circle to the essence of our stories. After thousands of years of human politics and blinding ignorance of the natural laws of our universe, we can finally re-address the original questions.

Who are we and how did we get here?

Notes

Chapter 17

A Challenge to Prevailing Ontology and Epistemology

"The world in which you were born is just one model of reality. Other cultures are not failed attempts at being you; they are unique manifestations of the human spirit."

—Wade Davis
anthropologist, ethnobotanist, and author

"At the end of an unsettling conversation with Socrates, Laches had a 'conversion' (metanoia), literally a 'turning around.' This did not mean that he had accepted a new doctrinal truth; on the contrary, he had discovered that, like Socrates himself, he knew nothing at all. Socrates had made him realize that the value system by which he had lived was without foundation; as a result, to go forward authentically, his new self must be based on doubt (aporia) rather than certainty. The type of wisdom that Socrates offered was not gained by acquiring items of knowledge but by learning to *be* in a different way." (Armstrong 2009)

How do we learn to *be* in a different way, so we can become new observers, as did Laches? Which brings us back to the key question of ontology: what does it mean to *be*?

It would help to remember that our scientific and religious belief systems—like all belief systems—although powerful, are social constructions. They are the result of our limited understanding of our reality. We might be able to live more fully if we are willing to live in the questions. To do so, we must be prepared to face the anxiety of admitting we do not know anything for certain. Only then will we keep learning.

This question then looms: keep learning what? Implicit in this question is the need to reconsider the source of what we consider valid information, our epistemology. To keep learning, as a process toward a different state of being, (ontology) means we must sort the wheat from the chaff—determine the validity of new knowledge. More concisely, decide what new information we accept and which we ignore?

In the case of religions, we probably should accept the original, universal human aspirations contained therein. They are valuable. Even though the path has been rugged and indirect, they have guided humankind on the trajectory to becoming better civilizations in most instances. More pointedly, the superstitious, magical, and wishful thinking that permeate our ancient texts and traditions (i.e., politically manipulated, multiply translated sacred texts, talking snakes, burning bushes, and arks full of animals) need to go, but not the wisdom. These superstitions are the usual culprits when we see human truths being disregarded while misguided people twist and turn passages and phrases to achieve their agendas or at the worst, justify their vilest emotions.

"In our society, rational discussion is often aggressive, since participants are not usually battling with themselves but doing their best to demonstrate the invalidity of their opponents' viewpoint." (Armstrong 2009) So, while antagonists are invalidating each other's viewpoints, and as Laches learned, the only valid supportable viewpoint is: I do not know.

Beyond these exercises in futility, we might open up to a faith that there is no *Truth* to be found. First, it would help to recognize and cure our addiction to concrete answers. No one knows the full extent of objective reality, our universe.

In Freeman Dyson's book, *Infinite in All Directions*, he offers a quote from a lecture by Emil Wiechert[79] speaking in 1896: "The universe is infinite in all directions, not only above us in the large but also below us in the small. If we start from our human scale of existence and explore the content of the universe further and further, we finally arrive, both in the large and the small, at misty distances where first our senses and then our concepts fail us."

We are proving this every day. Even with the theory of the Big Bang, we plainly are not certain of how the Universe got here. We have theories that explain what happened immediately after the bang but the cause of the specific event and what preceded it remain a mystery. Has the universe existed for all time? Is it infinite? More importantly, is there an intentional agent, "God," or merely increasing entropy, punctuated by complex structures organized by and explained with natural laws? We will not find new answers from our viewpoint of already knowing. Especially from those viewpoints whose origins date back three thousand years to desert tribes living in the Bronze Age.

We need an updated understanding of what it means to be a human being in the twenty-first century. In other words, a new ontology. Moreover, the study of UCE's in selected parts of near death experiences just might help us develop one.

While we are making progress in understanding our universe and our physical makeup, we are having a difficult time changing our beliefs about who we are beyond our physiology. In fact, we are drifting dangerously close to believing when we fully identify all the components of our biological systems, we will have explained human life in its entirety.

This is simply insufficient. We know the science of genetics does not provide a complete explanation. Our consciousness and subjective experiences have proven to be too complex to be explained by the biological components of our bodies.

Yes, we can identify which parts of our brains are at work as we experience our reality, but we still rely on ancient beliefs about the meanings of those experiences. So far, the scientific method does not bring clarity to the very human question: What does this all mean, if anything? For that, we have looked to our philosophies, in the context of this book, one of its forms, religions.

Our religions contain premises and beliefs based on the primitive explanations in our ancient texts, which in turn seem to have been influenced by NDE's. The present simplified forms are a result of human manipulation, errors, political ambitions, and every other kind of perversion possible. St. Augustine pointed to this when he supposedly said, "the Church is a whore, but she is our mother."[80] He may have meant although the religious story has been perverted by the history and used to advance personal and political agendas, he still had faith in the core teachings to show us underlying human truths.

On the one hand, we are trying to explain meaning by objective analysis and ignore subjective experience. On the contrary, we are honoring subjective interpretations and misinterpretations of ancient texts. These texts are the ones gleaned—from the many to the few—to advance ideological agendas. All this said we need a different understanding of what it means to *be*. This is not a new doctrinal truth to cling to, but a new way of being without knowing. We do not fully know much of anything for sure, let alone have the wherewithal to explain everything around us. As we have seen, we only perceive a minute portion of everything around us.

The first step toward a new ontology is to investigate its epistemological basis, i.e., the knowledge base that supports it. In other words, what knowledge do we consider valid in its construction? Much of our current science is based on the ontology that leans in the direction of explaining our brains as Turing Machines,[81] a purely algorithmic processor that stores, retrieves, and manipulates objective facts and data.

In this way, knowing more means gathering more facts and data because they are the only valid information, which, of course, can be only attained by the scientific method of objective reduction and analysis of the evidence. In other words, knowledge is advanced mostly by collecting more empirically derived data.

If we only depend on one kind of knowledge—which we think we know—either religious or scientific, we are limited by our pre-existing and incomplete logic, unexamined presuppositions and impoverished explanations of what it means to be human. When we do this, we run the risk of simply rearranging our prejudices and premises with no substantive difference in the outcomes. We are rearranging our presuppositions without expanding our previous epistemology and calling it thinking.

In this case, the debate between faith and reason will continue unabated and unresolved because the debate is based on the validity of differing sources of knowledge, which form the contexts: the different contexts of the two poles of rationalism and empiricism.

We need to be like Laches, whom Socrates helped to have a conversion. Not to a new doctrinal truth, but to a new way of being, in a way that opened him up to the discovery of new knowledge. This conversion happened because Socrates was able to disprove Laches' arguments until no grounding remained. In the face of this vacuum, he had to admit he knew nothing with certainty.

If we can admit we do know much but nothing with certainty, we might create an opening to allow new learning from the poles of both epistemologies. This will require faith. However, first, it will need a willingness to examine how we know what we *think* we know.

We will need a different kind of faith

The late Jesuit priest, Anthony De Mello's remarks, "It's like looking at one of the wonders of the world. That is faith! An openness to the Truth, no matter what the consequences, no matter where it leads you."

Laches' conversion required a simple faith in the unknowable, and so does ours. If we are to understand the essence of what it means to be human, we cannot simply remain open to new questions; we must question the knowledge from which our questions emerge.

Even more importantly, we must learn a new way to know and not completely depend on empirical data from objective investigation. We have proven its failure to provide comprehensive explanations to our questions. It has shown its limits. Of course, we will encounter the natural human resistance to any change; we want to have better answers, be more effective, but we do not want to change our point of view. We want to remain the observers we are and have the world change to fit. We somehow want **it** to happen to us exactly as **we** are; exactly how we observe our world; to maintain our current world view. It cannot be done.

To have new answers, we need new questions; to have new questions, we need to be different observers. To be new observers, we must jettison our *absolute* belief in the validity of the knowledge we use to form our assessments. This means questioning what we already believe.

We are the co-creators of reality

Paul Davies, professor of physics and cosmology at Arizona State University, offers us a clue to another ontology. First, he proposes we are special, as we play a vital function. As others have pointed out, in fact, we are interwoven within the process of the universe.

Our consciousness has emerged from the natural functioning of indeterminate processes. Yet, our consciousness is necessary for the universe to unfold as it is. We and the universe are in a kind of feedback loop. We clarify its fuzziness that we find at the most fundamental level of nature—the phase space of the quantum world— a space of pure probability. How this all started is beyond my ability to comprehend. The nagging paradox is the need for an observer to reduce the actual from the probability at the foundation of reality. Who, where, or what was the observer that started it all?

Professor Davies goes on to explain that we even clarify how the universe functions as we do our research and find that natural laws only become this way because we observe them to be this way. In other words, even the potential for the natural laws of the universe exists in undifferentiated phase space waiting to be clarified by our observations. We are critical in the discovery, explanation, and unfolding of the universe and it in us.

How are we so powerful?

To understand his proposition, we must examine the transparent premises, the foundation, supporting it. First, we must remind ourselves that at the fundamental–quantum level of our universe, everything exists as a probability. In other words, an infinite number of possibilities exist. When we observe them, we reduce the infinite to the finite. We bring them into the actual 3D classical level of reality. In this way, we are making a finite reality out of infinite possibilities. We are co-creating the world we consider real.

Think of this phenomenon like creating an oil painting: bringing a work of art into existence from a blank canvas. Each personal experience is a brush stroke that creates the final product. None of the brush strokes alone would make sense to us, but when added together we see the completed forms, colors, and textures.

We even define history. Consider the modern-day news story. The event happens, but the ways of observing it seem limitless. We can see this by reading and hearing about it from the participants, direct observers, and all the various perspectives of the people in the news business. No wonder the newspaper has been called the "first draft of history."[82]

Of course, we cannot ignore the best example. Our politics consists of revised and re-revised observations of the supposedly same situations. Given our propensity to think our point-of-view is the exclusive truth, we have the polarity we now experience. We see only our own brush strokes and insist our incomplete view constitute the entire finished work of art.

Religion is one of our topics, and it does not take much discernment to see its weaknesses at work in our postmodern religious belief systems. Contemporary religions have carved out certain specifics from infinite probabilities and made them into certain beliefs that demand complete faith. Humanity has painted the picture of religion with the help of billions, but some of us insist on seeing only our personal brush strokes.

It should be obvious by now these stories are not consistent with our current understanding of our natural functioning in the universe. They can be better understood on a different epistemological basis that creates a more complete and more valid context. The serious study of authentic near death experiences offers us an opportunity for just such an expanded epistemological foundation.

In summary, if there is meaning to human life, it might be discovered when we recognize our consciousness as the vehicle to the co-creation of the universe. Consciousness is our ground of being. We are the individual artists. The universe is our canvas. We are co-creating it as we live our lives. When we stop discovery, we stop painting new art on the canvas of human experience. When we maintain a stubborn and blind faith in our beliefs, our art project is not finished: It is simply abandoned.

This is the basis for a different ontology. It cannot be developed within the limitations of our current epistemological biases for empirical evidence or superstitious beliefs alone. We might be seeing the door opening to new ways of understanding what it means to be sentient in a universe of such mystical proportions.

Notes

Chapter 18

Individuals as Observers

"The real voyage of discovery consists not in seeking new landscapes, but in having new eyes."

—Marcel Proust
French novelist, critic, essayist

What does it mean to be observers? The classical definition is *somebody, who observes some object or event that is happening.* Implicit in this definition is the premise that observers see things as *they* are. So, what is missing in this definition?

As observers, our observations are influenced first by our evolutionarily adapted neurophysiology and then by what we already believe, how we know it, and how we validate and invalidate new information. In other words, our personal cognitive maps of reality determine what we believe and see. Alternatively, as Kathleen Taylor calls them in her book, Brainwashing: The science of thought control, "cogwebs, a generic term for mental objects, incorporating cognitive networks and schemas, thoughts, concepts, beliefs, hopes, desires, action plans and so on."

Our natural tendency is to think the world is fully explained by our incomplete cogwebs as though they are whole and complete. These cogwebs come to life in the ongoing narrative in our minds. That's the same narrative I mentioned in the introduction to this section of the book.

In our complex world, these simple cognitive devices limit our possibilities by interpreting our current experiences with the presuppositions contained in our internal narratives. We may not be able to expand them to see all reality, but we can expand them. As cognitive scientists are now proving, our maps are not the territory, and they form our limitations to seeing more territory. Keep in mind that much of the content of our cogwebs is grounded in language, and we have already seen the limitations we experience because we live in our linguistic houses of being. When we accept these facts, it can be the beginning of our voyage of discovery. In other words, this can be the beginning stage of becoming a new observer. Of it will take effort just to overcome our natural tendency to believe what we think without questioning.

So, exactly what is a new observer? Well, it is not another person. As Proust points out, it is the same person with the ability to see the same reality as though with new eyes.

For instance, some of us will view certain portions of an NDE as an unexplained consciousness event. Some will see it as the last bodily reaction to the process of dying. Some will view it as an aberration that simply can't be explained. Some will consider it a hoax being played to get attention. Each different view is based on the cogwebs that are unique to the observer.

An Example of a New Observer

A simple example of the new observer would be the pre-historic individual who saw that a form of transportation could come from a continually rotating object. Voila, the wheel! Rocks, logs, etc., rotating objects had been around for a long time, but this primitive human saw them as though with new eyes.

Another example is when Copernicus observed that the sun and universe did not revolve around Earth and gave us what is known as the heliocentric scientific explanation that opened a whole new level of understanding of our cosmos to be studied. In effect, these are the events when someone sees the same *reality* everyone else sees but sees it differently. When they do, a new paradigm is born and that allows new choices to emerge and create a whole new range of entirely new possibilities.

With each new observation comes the tug and pull of resistance from other people. There are those who take advantage of the opportunities emerging from new insights, and there are those, who are certain only ruin can come in their wake. Unfortunately, the new eyes Proust refers to almost always come with a need for safety glasses.

172

From the beginning of written history to our post-modern conflicts between conservatives and progressives, the struggle between opposing and transformative forces defines our species, both internally and externally. We seem always to be in a state of asymmetry, somewhat like a giant tug-of-war. Each side pulls the other toward the center until critical mass is reached and we move on – most of us do – some will die before they change their minds. Fortunately, for our species, these new observers eventually prevail and we make progress, or we might still think Earth is the center of the universe.

"The plain fact is different observers, operating with different sets of distinctions, see different realities. Notice that we aren't saying (as our rationalistic scientific common sense wants us to) that one reality is true and the other false. In each case, each observer sees what he/she sees, and this is what is real for him/her. One observer may have more refined or sophisticated distinctions than the other according to certain standards, but this doesn't make him/her right and the other person wrong.

"We can recognize this very clearly if we think about an astrologer looking at the identical night sky as the astronomer. The astrologer will see a completely different set of groupings, noting perhaps that a certain planet is in a certain astrological house, and so forth. Neither is right or wrong. They are simply motivated by different purposes, operating with different sets of distinctions based on different systems of thought, and, as a result, seeing different worlds.

"The observer is generative: that is, we actually create the reality we cognize, and thus determine what constitutes knowledge for us. In other words, what we know depends on what distinctions we already have, which is to say, on the kind of observer we are." (Olalla 2004)

Herein is one of the greatest obstacles to understanding UCE's, NDE's in particular, and the fundamental nature of the universe. We don't have the new distinctions to cognize or represent the reality we are observing when examining them. We are using existing distinctions that don't apply. Brian Greene, a contemporary theoretical physicist and author, says it best: "Surely, reality is what we think it is; reality is revealed to us by our experiences. To one extent or another, this view of reality is one that many of us hold, if only implicitly. I certainly find myself thinking this way in my day to day life; it's easy to be seduced by the face nature reveals directly to us […] "I've learned that modern science tells us a very different story. The overarching lesson that has emerged from scientific inquiry over the last century is that human experience is often a misleading guide to the true nature of reality. […] By deepening our understanding of the true nature of our physical reality, we profoundly reconfigure our sense of ourselves and our experience of the universe. (Greene 2004)

The point I'm making is many of our observations and perceptions, even our consciousness, is derived from what we already know. And what we already know is a very small, incomplete portion of reality, that tiny human work of art on the infinite canvas. And to make it even more limiting, the reality we know is known only to us as we co-create it in interaction with the universe.

As I've written in previous chapters, we are only one part of a chain of life that has existed for millions of years. Every niche in that chain required a level of consciousness to co-create it before we could even exist. If you think about it the next time you take a walk, thank the ants, insects, birds, all the other species who participate the web of consciousness that built what we call life.

How Much Do We Know?

As I wrote earlier in this book, professor of cognitive science, Dr. Donald Hoffman, has shown we have evolved to be evolutionary fit and but not have the ability actually to perceive the true nature of our universe. Now Dr. Marcus E. Raichle, a neurologist at Washington University, makes our experience of reality a bit more tenuous as he explains our perceptive capacity: "Such a thin stream of data could not produce perception if that were all the brain took into account; the intrinsic activity must play a role."[83]

In broad strokes, he is helping paint a picture that says we just don't have much of a grasp of the reality that we fight so hard to defend. Our experience depends a great deal on intrinsic activity. The substance of this intrinsic activity is our previous experience formed into those cogwebs mentioned earlier. We only perceive a tiny portion of the world around us. This tiny portion of our perceived world is screened and interpreted with what we already know and believe. What we already know and believe is the result of our previous highly-filtered perceptive abilities contained in our internal narratives. New information is always modified and fit to our internal cognitive ecology-our maps.

Then the intrinsic activity is coded into linguistic distinctions we call words.[84] These linguistic distinctions are one of the building blocks of our cognitive models[85] expressed in our internal narratives. In the simplest terms, we can understand linguistic distinctions this way: The dictionary is a book of linguistic distinctions, which, when each is understood, defines a tiny granular piece of our shared reality. If you do not know what a word means, you do not possess this distinction and, therefore, cannot fully understand this little piece of our shared reality. The process of learning linguistic distinctions is a step in our cognitive development. Think of how a child develops a functioning vocabulary to be able to communicate and interact with others.

An example might help. If you've never been on a sailboat and were invited to take your first trip, you might see neatly organized *ropes*. However, after being taught the role of each of these "ropes" as jib sheets, mainsheets, halyards, and docking lines, you would be learning a new set of linguistic distinctions that now allow you to experience that same reality differently. As a new observer, you would learn the function of each type and have a more thorough grasp of how the boat functions. Then you would understand the old sailor's maxim, "there are no ropes on sailboats."

On the other hand, you might just enjoy the ride and not worry about what each of these *ropes* does. Moreover, that is a legitimate position to take. However, if you wanted to be effective at sailing, you would need to learn these distinctions. As is all of life, more distinctions give you the ability to be more effective. In other words, the more open your system of knowledge, the more effective you will be. (Simply taking the time to read a few words in the dictionary every day can open up whole new panoramas of awareness.)

To study UCE's, our systems of knowledge must be more open than they are. We live in closed systems of knowledge because they, like a dictionary, are usually circular, self-referential systems. Closed systems do not distinguish, let alone, ask the questions we need to have answered. We need only examine the societal spasms around this troubled world, to see old models do not work to create new questions, let alone provide answers.

We are now experiencing the ineffectiveness of the observers who preceded us. Not only because we do not have the right answers, but also because we may not know the right questions to ask. The previous models that created the current problems do not contain the questions that would allow the correct answers. If we are not able to ask the right questions of people who experience UCE's we will never learn their true nature. Moreover, the search may end there. If so, we run the risk of ignoring what could be the most important discovery of our time; ability to experience our true nature and that of the universe full of possibilities we had not imagined. Not the description of our reality so filled with confusion, disputes, and endless wars, but the true nature described by theoretical physicists and all the great prophets of our species.

As troubled as the world is now, we are at a time of great opportunity. Very few people would argue with the statement "the world is plagued with constant breakdowns." If only we grasp this fact and see the opportunities that abound.

How could a breakdown be a great opportunity?

The end of the effectiveness of a cognitive map is what Martin Heidegger[86], a twentieth-century German philosopher, referred to as a type of breakdown in the transparency of living. Paradoxically, this transparency creates a kind of fog of unawareness. Breakdowns of this nature happen when we become aware of some subconscious aspect of our life because it is not working as it usually does. It is an interruption in our way of being.

Breakdowns in transparency are golden learning opportunities to become new observers. UCE's are just such breakdowns as are certain veridical NDE's that transform those who have them. If we examine them thoroughly, they can show us the failure of our beliefs, theories, premises, and ultimately, our logic. By seeing and questioning them, we can become different observers. If we do, we create new possibilities we could not see before. In this way, we can see that possibility has been there, but the observers we are, could not see them. Something is happening in UCE's that should wake us to a new level of observation.

In summary, we live our lives without conscious awareness of all its details. We have evolutionarily adapted perception that makes us fit for survival, but it does not reveal the full and complete truth of reality. We have a filtering ability allowing us to sift out millions of bits of input data and focus on the task at hand. This gift is also a limitation because it causes us to miss so much going on around us. In other words, our normal state is one of being conscious of a minuscule area; what we call awareness. The rest is transparent.

When transparency breaks down, we might become aware of whatever is causing the breakdown (e.g., a belief). If the issue is urgent, sometimes the events change our point-of-view, and we begin to see as though with new eyes, become new observers. If we're not curious or insist that our view is complete and certain, life returns to transparency, and we remain the same observer we have always been. However, the cost of this reluctance is often dearer than the effort to change. It is up to us.

Often, when there are serious breakdowns in the transparency of our lives we cling to what we have always believed until we just cannot hang on to it any longer. We take seemingly new actions, but they come from our existing point-of-view. They do not work; we try again. They continue not to work; we keep trying.

The key to new learning is the ability to question the observers that we are? In other words, questioning the way we see the situation causing the problem. A breakdown in transparency is a choice point— an opportunity to grow. When we use these opportunities, we can continue to expand our options. Instead of trying new actions repeatedly, trying to see the situation with new eyes may make all the difference we need to be more effective personally and as a species.

Notes

Chapter 19

Observers and Cognitive Maps

"The map is not the territory."

—Alfred Korzybski
Polish-born American engineer, mathematician, philosopher

As covered in the previous chapter, as observers we have developed cognitive maps that help us negotiate our worlds. They are models we use as short-hand methods of dealing with life and its complexities. UCE's don't fit within most socially and scientifically accepted maps of reality. However, Alfred Korzybski wrote something crucial, "The map (or model) is not the territory." He was telling us that our *cognitive maps*[87] or *models of the world*[88] are not the objective world. They work like any other map. They describe the territory but *are not* the territory. Maps are like the menu you use in a restaurant. It represents the food but is not the food.

Steven Hawking, English theoretical physicist, and cosmologist, and Leonard Mlodinow, physicists, and authors, in their book, *The Grand Design*, point to the same thing when they refer to "model-dependent realism." The term *model-dependent realism* not only describes how we all build cognitive maps of our worlds as we perceive them but how differing social constructions built on these different maps can be equally valid if they meet certain criteria.

Hawking and Mlodinow refer to a point relevant to my arguments when they say "models, that work, are equal in value."

In other words, the test of a model or map is its ability to provide full and complete explanations and to anticipate events with some degree of probability. If different cognitive maps can provide accurate, full, and complete explanations, then they are equally valid.

In Hawking's and Mlodinow's words, "there may be different ways in which one could model the same situation, with each employing fundamental elements and concepts. If two such [...] models accurately predict the same events, one cannot be said to be more real than the other; rather we are free to use whichever model is most convenient." (Hawking 2010)

So, when we say *real*, we are talking about something other than the map we use to describe it.

A good example of "another way to model a situation with different fundamental elements and concepts," is the story told in former evangelical Christian missionary, Daniel L. Everett's book, entitled, *Don't Sleep, there are Snakes*. It shows a real picture of how the cognitive models of a group of people live in a model-dependent reality very different from ours in modern industrialized societies. Yet, it resists interference and disruption. It works for the people of this tribe, which makes it valid in their circumstances.

In this book, Everett—then a Christian missionary—discovered that the Amazonian Pirahas Indians do not want or need the gospel of salvation. They are not interested in our deities. "They're missing one important belief that is required for their acceptance of a religion; that their life is incomplete without belief in some transcendent truth.

"Truth to the Pirahas is catching a fish, rowing a canoe, laughing with your children, loving your brother, dying of malaria. The Pirahas are firmly committed to the pragmatic concept of utility. They don't believe in a heaven above us or a hell below us, or that any abstract cause is worth dying for. They give us an opportunity to consider what a life without absolutes, like righteousness or holiness and sin could be like. And their vision is appealing." (Everett 2008)

This is their collective interpretation of reality, which shapes their cognitive maps, and it works for them. Their reality is closed to outside influences—it is a reality, which simply doesn't change. The Pirahas do not need new answers because they have few doubts that cannot be explained with their cognitive maps: no new questions, no need for new maps.

New questions come when we're faced with events that do not fit within our existing cognitive maps, like a UCE.

Which cognitive model truly represents the reality we all share, particularly if we acknowledge that something unexplainable is happening in an authentic NDE? In our Western logic, it would need to be one or the other, *A* or *not A*. Although cognitive maps are personal, they merge to create the social constructions making up our world of interpretations and explanations within which we live. In the U.S., we generally fall into one of two categories of maps, religious or scientific. Of course, there are others, but we are focusing on these two broad general categories because the major objections to NDE's as UCE's seem to fit these two most.

If we consider everyone's personal cognitive maps, including those who experience these events, will we not build more complete social constructions? When and if we do, will we be more able to understand ourselves and the universe we inhabit? Moreover, in doing so, will we be able to understand and explore UCE's more fully?

Korzybski, Hawking, Mlodinow, and many other authors who we have mentioned, agree that our sensory range, not only the specific five senses but also our neurology is not able to manage all of our sensory input. Which leads to the conclusion we do not experience the objective world as much as we experience an accumulation of our interpretations stored as memories based on perceptions filtered by our evolutionarily fit sensory systems. These are unique to each of us. In other words, these are our subjective cognitive maps, cogwebs if you prefer. This being the case, we have two sets of biological or bodily limitations; what we may refer to as reduction mechanisms, reducing sensory input to our central nervous system.[89]

The first set is our sensory system itself—seeing, hearing, tasting, smelling, and feeling—tactile[90] and visceral.[91] The second limitation is our inability to process nearly enough input to get well-formed and complete perceptions of the world around us. It is a component of the first: Our nervous systems have evolved to limit sensory information, filtering out what we do not need. All we can do is take sips of the firehose-like stream of information around us.

We have adapted to what British evolutionary biologist and author, Richard Dawkins, calls the *middle world*—a three-dimensional world between the infinitesimal subatomic and the unimaginably vast size of our universe.

In effect, we only have a thin stream of information coming in. We do not have direct experience of our world, but rather with our limited central nervous systems' responses to it in the form of our pre-existing and very subjective maps of reality. Everything we perceive is the result of internal interactions with our own neurological system that produce what is called qualia[92]. These are internal representations of external stimuli. Reread this sentence: We do not directly experience external reality. We experience our internally created qualia.

Now consider scientific and religious arguments. Based on uniquely different models, they attempt to explain the supposedly same situations. They employ many different fundamental elements and concepts. These are based on differing sources of knowledge, i.e., epistemologies. We call them truths; not only do we call them truths, but we will also argue, debate, and in the case of some religions, use physical violence and kill each other in their defense.

Given the fact our cognitive maps merge to become our social constructions, deconstruction and reconstruction are not only desirable but imperative. Scientist, Albert Einstein, warned of our limitations when he said, "We cannot solve problems by using the same kind of thinking we used to create them."

Does this mean everything our personal maps or models possess is wrong? Of course not, but it is a sure bet they are woefully incomplete. In other words, we need to question our models to create *new* questions if we are to find the answers that exist outside of their range of explanations. And for most of us, NDE's as UCE's fall outside our range of explanations.

All models are needed to understand the world we live in together. In other words, we will learn more if we respect not only scientific explanations but also validate subjective experience, rationalism, as a legitimate method in our investigations. If we are going to understand all authentic UCE's, we must honor the subjective experience of those who have them.

In summary, we are the flashes of conscious awareness that, when combined, illuminate the universe. In this metaphor, a single lightning flash cannot illuminate the entire area. No single map contains a comprehensive description of the whole universe and its mysteries. It takes us all to create the reality within which we function. We can learn from everyone's map because we all have representations of our so-called objective reality that are not a whole and comprehensive picture. If we take this seriously, we will generate new questions.

However, first, we need to question our dearest answers. Absolute faith in the belief systems of science and religion stops us from doing this.

We love our answers. Thus, the world is embattled around the issue of whose truth is the Real Truth. Religious truth is grounded in re-interpreted and revised, incomplete models of reality created in a time of significant scientific and philosophical ignorance. Science treats subjective experience with suspicion and claims the only valid answers are those supported by empirical evidence—only if such proof can repeatedly be reproduced. Neither model is whole and complete.

So, if we accept Korzybski's admonition, the map is not the territory, we need new maps to explore new territory.

Notes

Chapter 20

Faith in What?

"Faith is not contrary to reason."

Sherwood Eddy, American author

Faith is at the beginning and the end of reason. Without faith, there would be no religion or science. We define faith as belief without logical proof. Scientific inquiry starts, not with logical proof, but with observation and curiosity. If we did not have faith that there is something deeper to be discovered about our observations, why would we look?

All observations are subjective, so science starts and ends with subjectivity even though the scientific method is called objective. Although this approach is effective, it fails to recognize and consider all possible sources of knowledge. Therefore, it must limit our understanding of ourselves and the universe.

To advance our knowledge, wouldn't it be better to reconsider subjective experience as a legitimate tool in our investigations? The reason is simple: investigation benefits from more, rather than less information. Summarily invalidating one closed system of knowledge with criteria established in another closed system of knowledge is illogical. It ultimately forms a dark space between the two systems. We get what we referred to earlier as the opposite poles of our epistemology. We never fully understand the larger context of our questions and answers.

The Power of Context

Any serious question exists within and must be posed and investigated in its context. When we derive our questions from a limited knowledge of their context, the answers might sound logically consistent and mislead us. A comprehensive understanding of a context will provoke better questions and provide better answers.

Therefore, we don't go to physicians for financial advice or barbers for auto repairs.

In the last one hundred years or so, we have become increasingly dependent upon the scientific method to explain the unknown. It has served us well in this regard. That said, for science to answer all its questions, it must have full knowledge of the context, within which, these questions arise. It does not. For instance, there remain whole areas of phenomena where current scientific thinking fails. So, it has limitations like any other closed system of logic.

For instance, our search for other life forms is limited because we are only aware of what constitutes life on earth and more specifically, only that which we can perceive as alive. We cannot fully explain the life forms on our planet, yet. We recently discovered life in places on earth where we never suspected life could evolve. One finding has defied the basic biological foundations upon which we have understood life and its origins. In this case, arsenic is alleged to be a functioning component in the physical makeup of a bacteria.[93] Obviously, arsenic is a poison to the rest of known life on the planet.

We can hardly comprehend the vast distances and seemingly infinite numbers of bodies—galaxies, stars, planets—in our cosmos. We can only partially explain the matter and energy in the universe. We know roughly 68 percent of the Universe is dark energy. Dark matter makes up about 27 percent. The rest - everything on Earth, everything ever observed with all our instruments, all normal matter - adds up to less than five percent of the Universe.

In other words, 95 percent of the universe remains a mystery. If 95 percent of the universe remains a mystery and this mystery is the background context within which scientific questions emerge, how can science answer its questions with complete certainty? The scientific method is dependable for answering questions with its models, which reinforces its context. However, 95 percent of its model remains a mystery.

As an example, our best theory, superstring theory requires ten dimensions to make sense. We can experience three physical and one time dimension. Could those other dimensions somehow be hidden in that 95 percent of the universe we do not yet understand?

Another, we still have not unified the four basic forces we know exist. We still have questions about gravity, even though we recently discovered gravitational waves and validated Einstein's explanation of gravity.[94]

And why is the universe expanding at a counter-intuitive accelerating rate? Although, our most recent thinking suggests it is because of dark energy; the same dark energy we still do not understand. However, if our calculations are correct, the power of dark energy would blow the universe out of existence.

We cannot fully correlate gravity at the cosmic level and the nuclear strong and weak forces at the level of subatomic particles. We find phenomena at the subatomic particle level that defies classical logic. We simply cannot understand it using our best rational thinking.

We still debate the existence of a grand unifying theory to explain classical physics and the quantum world of subatomic particles. We do not yet fully explain how the universe can function with phenomena at these two levels observing entirely different physical laws. There exists a division, even in the world of theoretical physicists; those, who believe there is no unifying theory to be found and those who believe a unifying theory exists.

We have only just begun to understand scientifically the possibility of the actual existence of our universe (i.e., Why was there more *matter* than *antimatter* left over from the "Big Bang"?) enough to evolve into this universe. Further, some scientists still question the "Big Bang" theory. For instance, how can everything that exists in the universe have fit into a tiny object smaller than a golf ball? According to cosmologist and theoretical physicist, Sean Carroll, the structure would have been so ordered; even an infinitesimally minute disorder would have produced a black hole instead of this universe.

The required level of order implies a deep, intelligent influence. This level of order does not randomly occur in our world. To be clear, I'm not advocating for a belief in an intelligent designer, but rather a deep and unexplainable force, intelligence, or logic, we have yet to discover–or may never discover. We live in a place we can barely apprehend, let alone fully comprehend. In Einstein's words, it is a universe of the subtle, intangible, and inexplicable. Yet, we and it are here.

Even though some believe in a unified universal theory and some do not our natural human curiosity and faith drive us to continue to explore. This exploration has been made more complicated considering our discovery of the quantum. Some physicists question whether we will ever explain it all.

According to Brazilian physicist and astronomer, Marcelo Gleiser: "Another group that would commit to Planck's[95] view are the believers in a hidden code of Nature, a set of fundamental laws and principles that describe the essence of physical reality. This code has many names. Familiar ones are "Final Theory" or Theory of Everything." The finality here implies two things that I find surprising: first, that there is an end to the search; second, that we humans can get there. I strongly disagree with both." (M. Gleiser 2010)

Richard P. Feynman, the 1965 Nobel Prize in Physics winner, explained why we must continue to investigate: "Every scientific law, every scientific principle, every statement of the results of an observation is some kind of summary which leaves out the details, because nothing can be stated precisely."[96]

This limitation exists in the scientific model because it is a human construction. Now, new discoveries contradict many of our previous scientific models. We are being forced to consider new information; to stretch the boundaries and re-structure the models. This is exactly the process that took us from Newtonian physics to Einstein's relativity to quantum mechanics. This is a time of what philosopher of science, Thomas Samuel Kuhn[97] called: a paradigm shift.

We know in matters of science and religion; we cannot take the human out of the equation because these are human inventions. As we learn more, we can *re-invent* each of them. Science is doing this with limited evidence from its own domain of inquiry. Certain contemporary religions are not. Some are becoming more radical in their re-interpretations, more extreme in their intransigence.

Their obstacle seems to be a stubborn faith in existing beliefs in the face of contradictory evidence. When we question our blind faith in religious and scientific beliefs, we open ourselves to the issue of faith in the unknowable. This is faith that trusts in what will come without the implied certainty of our religious or scientific theories. It is the faith that allows new inquiry.

Ultimately, we must finally resort to faith. Faith that natural laws and order, when found, will further our knowledge of the deeper mysteries of the universe. Faith that there is a deeper reason a universe that tends toward increasing chaos produces complex organized entities in an orderly manner at the classical level.

This whole idea of faith comes from a basic understanding that human knowledge is limited. Without faith in something, our continuing search for the answers would not make sense. Now, we are engaged in the atheist book wars. Daniel Dennett, Richard Dawkins, the late Christopher Hitchens, and Sam Harris have all offered us their reasons for atheism. However, these admittedly educated and intelligent people do not make incontrovertible arguments. The reason is these arguments are based on the only logic available to them: human logic.

We base our logic on our limited common sense experience of our natural world. We all live in limited social constructions we call reality. So, all our arguments are bound up within closed and incomplete systems, which so far have not proven or disproven the deep intelligence of the universe.

In summary, science honors empirical evidence and suspects subjectivity. Religion ignores empirical evidence and honors subjectivity. Ninety-five percent of the universe remains a mystery. It seems that to understand the mystery; a more effective search strategy should include both methods. While reductive scientific analysis can describe and explain the components of its subject, it cannot fully explain the emergent properties of these parts; the whole.

Subjective experience is part of the whole. In this way, subjective investigation must be a part of our explorations of the whole of life and the universe. So, while we struggle to figure out the natural world, we are left to speculate about what some of us have called supernatural. The limitation is us. It is our limited ability to experience anything outside of the classical level—our earthly experiences shaped by our evolution.

Our experience is limited by our physiology (i.e., it is embodied).[98] Our reasoning is limited to this embodiment. We simply cannot explain what falls out of our ability to understand in human metaphorical and mathematical terms.

Even though our ability to mathematically define and prove many levels of existence we cannot perceive, we are only scratching the surface of our incomprehensible cosmos. We do not know what lies beyond. In this regard, religion claims to start where science ends; itself an attempt to provide an explanation with its own limitations.

Finally, we are left with nothing but faith. Faith, that if we keep investigating, we will eventually be rewarded for our efforts. There are much deeper mysteries to be discovered.

Notes

Chapter 21

Summarizing: Our Need for Reunion of Self, Science, and Philosophy.

"Human beings are the only creatures we know who are incomplete. Rocks will never be more or less flinty; carrots will never be more or less vegetable; cows will never be more or less bovine. But humans are free to be more—or less—human. Witness the vast spectrum that separates Dr. Josef Mengele from Dr. Albert Schweitzer."

—William J. O'Malley, S.J.
American Jesuit priest, author

The Origins of Separation

In the earliest stages of becoming "more—or less—human," we became conscious beings. Admittedly, some of us were, and still are, more conscious than others. During the evolution of our consciousness, two critical questions emerged: Who are we? What is this place?

For centuries, the undifferentiated human search to answer those questions was called *philosophy*. It focused on matters such as existence, knowledge, values, reason, mind, and language.

According to Bernard d'Espagnat, French physicist, science philosopher, and author of *On Physics and Philosophy*: "The continued use of this old acronym, Ph.D., even for a scientist, reminds us that until the seventeenth or eighteenth century, science and philosophy were hardly separate, that people such as Descartes, Pascal, and Leibniz were brilliant in both, in short, that most prominent thinkers did not shun mixing scientific and metaphysical research." (d'Espagnat 2006)

Science Then Branched from Philosophy:

"Eventually, this split could be summarized as having philosophers be concerned with problems bearing on the nature of things and scientists with those problems bearing on their behavior." (d'Espagnat 2006)

Until this point, we shared a common epistemology, the branch of philosophy that investigates the origin, nature, methods, and limits of human knowledge.

In effect, we accepted the validity of subjective experience and objective evidence. "These two models of human thinking, termed rationalism and empiricism, respectively, formed the major intellectual legacy of the West, down to Descartes and Bacon, who in the seventeenth century, represented, the twin poles of epistemology."[99]

These epistemological differences, sources of knowledge, defined the space of this inquiry. In particular, by how they are reflected in the study of faith. Why faith? Because faith is belief without evidence and it has the potential to stop all progress in learning. And most of us have a great deal of faith in what we already believe. I pointed out that when faith in our beliefs becomes strong enough, it becomes an ideology and all discussion ends.

Remember, it is important to note that ideology comes in many forms. Our immediate interpretation usually goes to religion as the ideology that stops discovery. While this is true in some instances, science too can become so ideological that even it can stop discovery.

So we are left with the question of who to believe when it comes to events as unusual as UCE's in general and NDE's in particular. And how this phenomenon might cast light on our understanding of the mysteries of the universe being revealed today.

Whom can we believe?

Is it the supposedly objective observer who denies the validity of a UCE even though indisputable evidence is offered? Alternatively, is it the person having the UCE or the NDEr who has faith in the reality of their near death experience? Neither option satisfies us. We might find more useful answers when we question the validity of both to explore what lies in the middle of these two poles. However, first, we must be able to confront those ideological obstacles, be they religious or scientific.

Until then, we have two decidedly limited search areas for new discoveries: (1) *Empiricism*: the belief that knowledge and investigation based on empirical evidence derived by the scientific method will eventually explain everything. So far it has not been successful in fully explaining NDE's, let alone a grand unifying theory or what constitutes 95 percent of our cosmos. (2) *Rationalism*: religious interpretations and revisions that allow no questioning even when facts contradict a personal point of view, for instance, a firmly held religious belief.

The good news is so far both have been useful in disqualifying the fake NDEr's who report an experience to get publicity. However, the proven fake reports are not our topic.

The Western Bias

In Western culture, we have been on a trajectory toward *scientism*, the belief that everything can be explained by the scientific method. Therefore, so much of the resistance to the acceptance of UCE's is based on a commitment to the scientific method based on a Newtonian/Einsteinian epistemology. Moreover, also, some religious people also refuse to accept the validity of UCE's, specifically NDE's because they do not fit into their literal interpretations of religious mythology; a mythology that does offer us clues as to the reality it tries to depict.

Why Science and Religion?

"Science and religion are two windows that people look through, trying to understand the big universe outside, trying to understand why we are here. The two windows give different views, but they look out at the same universe. Both views are one-sided, neither is complete.

Both leave out essential features of the real world. And both are worthy of respect.

"Trouble arises when either science or religion claims universal jurisdiction when either religious or scientific dogma claims to be infallible. Religious creationists and scientific materialists are equally dogmatic and insensitive. By their arrogance, they bring both science and religion into disrepute.

"The media exaggerate their numbers and importance. The media rarely mention the fact that the great majority of religious people belong to moderate denominations that treat science with respect or the fact that the great majority of scientists treat religion with respect so long as religion does not claim jurisdiction over scientific questions." (Freeman Dyson 1988)

Opening the Door to Reunification

"Now, something monumentally important has happened to cause a significant disruption to the trends toward the *infallibilities* of science and religion. Great philosophical riddles lie at the core of present-day physics and most people, by now, are aware of their existence, even if but a few have a precise idea of their nature. It is imperative nowadays that any tentative approach to a philosophical world view should take information coming from contemporary physics into account quite seriously." (d'Espagnat 2006)

What happened to prompt this advice from d'Espagnat, a professor emeritus of physics? As I have written throughout this book, the discovery of the quantum level of the universe happened. It shook the scientific method loose from its moorings and opened the door for reunification: It offers a new form of mutual inquiry into the original questions.

Again, we thank German physicist, scientist Max Planck (1858 – 1947) the father of the quantum theory, for which he received the 1918 Nobel Prize in Physics. His discovery shifted the way we think about the very essence of reality, which frames the core questions in science and religion. He offered this bit of wisdom that fits the topic of this book perfectly,

"I regard consciousness as fundamental. I regard matter as derivative from consciousness. We cannot get behind consciousness. Everything that we talk about, everything that we regard as existing, postulates consciousness."

His discovery of the quantum, not only challenged our logic, but it showed the insufficiency of the epistemology of empiricism as a final and absolute method of explaining the essence of our universe with mathematical certainty. In other words, the traditional scientific method had to be seen as an incomplete method for explaining our reality. Because we now know even classical mathematical certainty is questionable at the fundamental level of the universe. "It loses connection with the real world around the quantum level."[100] This math is the traditional math we have relied upon to provide what we call certainty at the *classical* level: the level of human experience.

However, even though our math fails at the quantum level, that level is the basis for everything that exists and we do co-create our objective reality from it. Our original theories told us it is made up of what we call matter and energy. Now we're not so sure. Moreover, even as scientists work to develop a deeper understanding, there is no comprehensive model for explaining it. As I pointed out earlier in this book, even the recent proof of the existence of the Higgs boson[101] at the Large Hadron Collider in Cern, Switzerland, left us with more questions.

Remember, since recent discoveries at the Large Hadron Collider, in Cern, Switzerland, two vital numbers cause theoretical physicists to question this model and ask the question, "have we reached the point where we must admit we cannot fully explain our universe?" To be clear, this is THE current model that provides the foundation for all the scientific cosmological theories of the universe for the last several decades.

This leaves us with two possibilities. The first is a difficult complex explanation: Superstring theories with 10 to the 500th power possibilities. A number so large it exceeds all the atoms in the universe and requires the existence of multiverses to be possible. This is a theory which cannot be tested with current technology. The second is an admission that the very basis for scientific explanations of our existence cannot be validated. Does this mean we have reached the limit of human understanding?

To be clear, the danger here is that someone will invoke the "god of the gaps" argument. That is not my purpose. My primary purpose is to argue that certainty is elusive – even with something as sacrosanct as the SMPP, the basis of the theories of particle physics.

In fact, it may simply be impossible to fully explain this universe scientifically. Yet, as the scientific method expands our knowledge of the cosmos, we have developed a rigid belief system that says, if science can prove it, it must be correct. These controversies should convince us it is more productive to live in the questions than to develop doctrinal truths that might mislead us.

As I pointed out earlier, every theory starts with human reasoning. Subjective thought is the first step to producing the objective evidence for any scientific model. So, every law, theory, hypothesis, and explanation of reality is ultimately subjective. Moreover, we have seen that all these theories are limited to our linguistic capabilities. Consequently, they depend upon a theoretical model created by humans; humans living in the confines of the House of Being that is our language.

Therefore, blind faith in scientific and religious beliefs limits discovery because they are both based on theory-dependent models of reality created by human beings and limited by language. Until we recognize this fact, we are collaborating to limit our knowledge, even as we search for more.

In fact, we cannot deny the authenticity of some UCE's and NDE's with the scientific method or contemporary religion.

In summary, if you've read this section, it is possible that scientific and religion's denials have not provided the sense of closure about UCE's or new discoveries in physics you need. This book did not provide all the answers. It is uncertain if this book offered some assurance, but perhaps your thinking about your place in the universe will change. Moreover, from there, hopefully, a whole new era of possibilities will emerge from reuniting the objectivity of science with the subjectivity of human experience.

This reunification may provide a remedy. This new way of thinking could end the alienation so obvious in the world today. We are not separate from each other and the universe. We are whole, connected, and complete. We are more than the biological components of our bodies.

Does this idea sound familiar? It should. The great prophets of the world have been telling us this for centuries. All we need to do is understand their teachings in a different context. A context that may not fit into our current understanding of reality. But maybe the very context we need if we are to survive as a species.

Notes

Epilog

There may be readers who still disagree with the speculations and proposals in this book. I think disagreement can be a positive force for learning. To produce new learning, disagreement is better served if it addresses the foundations of the argument that causes the disagreement. The following outlines my method and argument.

How We Are Fooled by Our Logic

Kurt Gödel, Austrian logician, mathematician, and philosopher, gave us his incompleteness theorems, which showed that a *consistent system,* one that contains no contradictions, [102] cannot prove the axioms that constitute the system. Therefore, there is a difference between what is provable within a system and what may be true apart from it.

To repeat, for logic to be consistent, it can contain no contradictions. For it to contain no contradictions, it must stay closed. So, any system of logic is a closed, consistent system. Closed, consistent or not, it is always a theory-dependent model, created by and limited to human theories. Science and philosophy, correspondingly, are logical systems that contain many internal disagreements.

We cannot call them consistent systems. We can say they both contain many different theory-dependent models that may prove their own axioms but not completely explain what may be true. In simple terms, a logical proof in either system is not necessarily evidence of *the whole truth.*

In this book, arguments have focused criticisms and propositions on the consistent system called Aristotle's logic of the excluded middle. You might know it as Boolean logic. Until the discovery of the quantum level, it has been the basis of analytical thinking in Western civilization. It is as prone to failure to reach conclusive evidence of *truths* as is any other closed system of thinking or belief.

Generally speaking, we do not question the logic that shapes our thinking. We reach conclusions based on unexamined presuppositions embedded in this logic, and as long as they seem logical, we assume they accurately explain the world around us. We are like fish in water—we live in our logic, unaware of its existence. However, if something happens that doesn't fit it, like a UCE, we usually discount it because it doesn't make sense in our system of thinking.

So, what do we do now? Maybe we should deconstruct the beliefs that inform our thinking. Why deconstruct beliefs? Because beliefs can be made apparent but are based on deeply embedded unexamined premises in our logic, which—as stated above—are transparent to us.

Just as a physician examines our vital signs for more information about how our bodies are functioning, we should examine the vital signs of our societies: our scientific and philosophical belief systems. That is if we are to discover the deeper failings of our logic.

This challenge is not easy. However, we must be aware that our thinking, although logical, is not necessarily correct. So when we encounter something as unusual as a UCE if we are not able to recognize that our logic and thinking are limited to pre-existing human theories and explanations, all new learning ceases.

What is Valid Information?

That said, the first step in our examination is to recognize the basis of what we consider being valid information, i.e. the core question of epistemology: In other words, how do we know what we know? Alternatively, what is the source of the information we consider valid? Until we open ourselves to other sources of valid information, we are bound to a single independent recursive system[103] of thinking. For the arguments in this book: either science or religion.

The specific area of religion I refer to is the practical philosophy of the masses, contemporary religion. In too many instances today, certain contemporary religions that prove themselves to be revisionist perversions of recursive systems. In other words, these two important domains of inquiry, science, and religion, are self-referential, meaning they depend on their own axioms to prove their axioms. Gödel showed they could not prove themselves. The question is, how can they disprove one another?

For the sake of this illustration, let's focus on the knowledge of these two important areas of human inquiry as contained in their texts. To try to deal with the millions of personal interpretations would be an impossible task. From the earliest to the most recent, our scientific texts contain the empirically derived evidence that makes up the whole body of scientific knowledge; not our wisdom. For that, we look to our philosophies; in some instances, the original forms of religions. So for this example, the focus of my critique is on the texts of these individual bodies of knowledge.

When we deconstruct our scientific and philosophical beliefs, we will find conflicting contradictory interpretations. We will also find that these conflicting interpretations are irreducible. We will end in a state of confusion.

The logic, presuppositions, and premises that make up our scientific and philosophical models are social constructions built on the illusion of internally logical foundations. They do not reflect *objective* reality in its entirety. Instead, they show that the reality we experience is a complex matrix of subjective interpretations validated by self-referential criteria. In Nietzsche's[104] words, "Our reality is made up of competing stories about reality."

If we can accept that our social reality is a sometimes coherent, mostly incoherent set of imaginary agreements, we can see that we have the capacity to re-imagine those that aren't working.

We need to question socially constructed reality. Develop new interpretations. Accept that all words are metaphors and serve as representations of something in our common experience. They are not the reality we experience but placeholders based on a common agreement made unconsciously as we are acculturated into our circumstances. Words not only describe but can and do change realities. The first and most important step in the process is to understand exactly how the core logic in Western civilization limits our understanding of the most basic level of our reality.

Our logic fails there. When we accept that fact, we see that it only creates the illusion of explaining our reality. This is not to say that quantum mechanics explains UCE's. It simply means that the logic we use to explain our reality as we experience it is not honored at the most fundamental level of the cosmos. If it doesn't work there, where else doesn't it work?

What is an Argument?

An argument is a line of reasoning or persuasive discourse. My argument follows: The disagreement at the epistemological poles is about the validity of knowledge and methods of discovery. To summarize, on the one hand, the only valid knowledge is that which can be confirmed with empirical evidence using the scientific method. On the other, the result of Descartes' radical skepticism: nothing is more reliable than subjective experience. This is precisely the fulcrum point of the disagreements about UCE's.

This disagreement not only limits our ability to develop comprehensive answers, but it also cast suspicions on our questions and investigative methods. Objective methods can only partially explain a subjective experience like a UCE. Science considers valid only those answers repeatedly proven with empirical evidence. However, science cannot provide a comprehensive explanation for everything. Consequently, these epistemologically limited answers cannot fully satisfy our key inquiry: what is our true nature and that of the universe? As Descartes showed us, subjective experience is pivotal in examining the question of our true nature.

Therefore, our questions and answers fail to examine fully the premises that inform another key element of our philosophical inquiry: our ontology, the study of existence: the most general branch of metaphysics, concerned with the nature of being.

The ontology of science and religion differ, so their questions emerge from a set of premises, which differ on the most elemental level: the nature of our being or existence. Again, the very core question that emerges as we study UCE's.

In the study of UCE's, neither system of thinking has been successful in the eyes of the other. They fail because (1) they each consider the validity of the other's knowledge with suspicion;(2) therefore, the ontology that forms each domain of inquiry remains incomplete; and (3) because their premises are based on recursive and, therefore, incomplete logic, now showing its shortcomings in the light of new discoveries of the true nature of the universe. Nonetheless, both have developed seemingly comprehensive belief systems, scientific and religious, which currently explain the universe as we think it is.

The key point here is because these belief systems are based on differing explanations of the nature of existence, we must first reconcile their ontological differences. To do this requires us to be open to a re-examination of what we consider being valid knowledge. So not only is there a lack of agreement on the fundamental basis of our existence, new scientific facts are now disrupting our theories of the underlying structure of our reality. This being so, shouldn't we re-think our way of understanding a UCE?

What Now?

With this dilemma facing us, we have no option, but to redirect our questions to:

What is valid knowledge?
How is this knowledge acquired?
How do we know what we know?

At the highest level, blind and unquestioning faith in our beliefs is bringing ruin to humanity and our planet. The original beliefs may have worked in the past, but they do not satisfactorily answer our questions about what it takes for us to sustain ourselves and our resources in the world's present state: an exponentially exploding population, currently over seven billion people.[105]

The rationale to re-examine our religious and scientific theories is that our logic has taken a shot amidships with the discovery of deeper levels of the universe. Our logic is insufficient to explain what we find there.

To be precise, the core logical syllogism that fails in our theories tells us something is or is not—it cannot be both. As strange as this seems, we became aware of this failure in our logic when we discovered how the universe functions at its most basic level. Things there don't obey the same laws that seem to organize reality at the level we can experience.

So knowing our logic is incomplete and may be contradictory, knowing that even the most logical way of human thinking, mathematics, does not work at the fundamental level of the universe, and knowing logic is the basis of our thinking. How can we not deconstruct the belief systems built on it?

What do discoveries at the quantum level of the universe have to do with us?

The quantum or *fundamental* level of the universe is not just out there somewhere in the vast space of the universe. It is the most fundamental substance of all reality, which means we, us, human beings, and our reality emerges from the quantum. Especially as we have already seen in this book, what we call our bodies and brains are spatial extensions of the quantum level.

According to the Nobel laureate, Francis Crick,

"To understand the brain, we may need to know the many interactions of nerve cells with each other; in addition, the behavior of each nerve cell may need explanation in terms of ions and molecules of which it is composed. Where does it end? Fortunately, there is a natural stopping point. This is at the level of chemical atoms [...] all the chemist needs to know about each atom is its nuclear charge in order to explain most of the facts about chemistry.

"To do this, he needs to understand the rather unexpected type of mechanics (called quantum mechanics) that controls the behavior of very small particles and electrons in particular and becomes impossibly intricate. In practice, since the calculations soon become impossibly intricate, he mainly uses various rules-of-thumb that we now see have reasonable explanations in terms of quantum mechanics. Below this level, he need not venture." (Crick 1994)

How Does This Knowledge Help Unify Us?

At the quantum level, the universe and we are all connected in a kind of holistic fabric—each of us to one another; each of us to the universe and everything in existence. When we realize our connection and the fact our logic is not honored at our basic level of our existence, shouldn't we begin to re-think our illusion of separation, not to mention the societal illnesses it causes?

If we can understand how we and the universe function on the most fundamental level, are we not empowered to re-think who we are and how we fit into this mysterious place we call the cosmos? Moreover, if we do, doesn't that open the door to examining the subjective experience of a UCE differently?

So thus far, we now know these two most important areas of human inquiry, science and religion are social constructions created by humanity based on a limited form of logic. We also know logical proofs, although consistent, are not necessarily true. And we know the split between religion and science has caused a disagreement about the essential features of knowledge (i.e., what methods of inquiry are valid and consequently, what is acceptable knowledge?)

These factors result in differing ontological foundations in science and religion. For instance, are we body and soul or just body? Consequently, they form a barrier to asking more comprehensive questions, which results in limited explanations, explanations that tend to gather around the epistemological poles of empiricism and rationalism, leaving the dark space between them: the general topics contained in this book.

These above limitations serve to hide premises not available without rigorous analysis, but at the surface level, their failure is evident everywhere. These are our stories. So why is this so important at this point in human history? They clearly no longer work to the benefit of our species and others in our web of life. Not only do they limit our ability to understand a near death experience but the evidence of their failure is all around us today: Miserable and unsustainable human conditions such as wars, terrorism, weapons of mass destruction, starvation, degradation of the planet, insatiable greed, failing institutions, government oppression, social and economic violence, and the despair and resignation of entire segments within many societies.

Even so, we should not ignore the contributions of these existing constructions up until lately. We have made enormous material progress due to science. We have made enormous intellectual progress due to philosophy, and religion in some forms. The extremes, scientism in science and fundamental revisionism in religion, are also making their contributions to human suffering.

In summary, we need a larger construction built upon a more unifying epistemology and logic that subsumes empirical evidence and subjective experience if we are to understand a UCE. We need a larger, more inclusive social construction to provide for the well-being of the individual, entire human race, and our planet. In other words, we need another look, not only at what we know but how we know what we know.

To this end, the epistemologies of science and religion are being challenged in this book so we can hopefully allow that something is going on in a UCE that might be most positive for the entire human race. I'm not offering what you just read as proof within either system. There are no doctrinal truths in this book. My interpretations hopefully, integrate, rather than separate. Many of these proposals are bizarre from a scientific and religious point-of-view. In effect, they might be both valid and invalid, much like the logic we find at the quantum level.

Discoveries of the quantum, consciousness studies, and near death experiences all offer us opportunities to re-think the societal ills that plague our species. However, first, we must be able to tolerate the stress that comes with changing our way of thinking to become new observers of the same reality we face every day. We have the power to unify ourselves and refuse to continue the devastation we are doing to our planet. Isn't it time we hold ourselves responsible?

Notes

Bibliography

(2007). In E. Kelly, *Irreducible Mind, Toward a Psychology for the 21st Century* (p. 416). Lanham, MD: Rowman and Littlefield.

Aikman, D. (2008). *The Delusion of Disbelief, why the New Atheism is a threat to your way of life.* Carol Stream, IL: Tyndale House Publishers, Inc.

Armstrong, K. (2009). *The Case for God.* New York, NY: Alfred A. Knorf.

Baggott, J. (2009). *A Beginner's Guide to Reality, exploriing our everyday adventures in wonderland.* New York, NY: Pegasus Books.

Carter, C. (2010). *Science and the Near-Death Experience: How Consciousness Survives Death.* Rochester, VT: Inner Traditions.

Crick, F. (1994). *The Astonishing Hypothesis, the scientic search for the soul.* New York, NY: Touchstone.

Damasio, A. (2010). *Self Comes to Mind, Contructing the Conscious Brain.* New York, New York: Pantheon Books.

De Mello, A. (1990). *Awareness, the perils and opportunities of reality.* New York, NY: Doubleday.

De Mello, A. (1990). *Awarenesss, the perils and opportunties of reality.* New York, NY: Doubleday.

DeFilippis, R. (2003). *You, your Self and the 21st Century.* Philadelphia, PA: Exlibris.

d'Espagnat, B. (2006). *On Physics and Philosophy.* Princeton, NJ: Princeton University Press.

Dyson, F. J. (1988). *Infinite in All Directions.* New York, Ny: Harper Perennial .

Edward R. Kelly, E. W. (2007). Irreducible Mind . Lanham, Maryland: Rowman and Littlefield Publishers, Inc.

Eisenstein, C. (2007). *The Ascent of Humanity.* Harrisburg, PA: Panenthea Press.

Everett, D. (2008). *Don't Sleep, There are Snakes, Life and language in the Amazonian Jungle.* New York, NY: Vintage Books.

Gallo, E. (1994). Syncronicity and the Archetypes. *The Skeptical Inquirer,* 18.

Gladwell, M. (2005). *Blink, The Power of Thinking Without Thinking.* New York, NY: Back Bay Books.

Gleiser, M. (2010, May 13). *13.7* . Retrieved May 14, 2010, from NPR: http://www.npr.org

Gleiser, M. (2010). *A Tear at the Edge of Creation.* New York, NY: Free Press.

Greene, B. (2004). *The Fabric of the Cosmos, space, time and the texture of reality.* New York, NY: Alfred Knorpf.

Greene, B. (2011). *The Hidden Reality.* New York, NY: Alfred A. Knopf.

Harris, S. (2010). *The Moral Landscape, how science can determine human values.* New York, NY: Free Press, a division of Simion & Schuster, Inc.

Hawking, S. &. (2010). *The Grand Design.* New York, NY: Bantam Books.

Herbert, N. (1985). *Quantum Reality, beyond the new physics.* Garden City, NY: Anchor Press/Double Day.

Hofstadter, D. R. (1979). *Godel, Escher, Bach, an eternal golden braid.* New York, NY: Basic Books, Inc.

Kaplan, M. (2009). *Bozo Sapiens.* New York, NY: Bloomsbury Press.

Kauffman, S. (2008). *Reinventing the Sacred.* New York, NY: Perseus Books Group.

Lakoff, G. &. (1999). *Philosophy of the Flesh.* New York, NY: Basic Books.

Long, J. (2010). *Evidence of the Afterlife, the science of near death experiences.* New York, NY: Harper Collins.

Meyer, M. (2007). *The Nag Hammadi Scriptures.* New York, NY: Harper Collins.

Mitchell, S. (1991). *The Gospel Accoring to Jesus.* New York, NY: Harper Collins.

Nelson, K. (2011). *The Spiritual Doorway in the Brain.* London, England: Dutton Press.

Olalla, J. (2004). *From Knowledge to Wisdom.* Boulder, CO: Newfield Network.

O'Malley, W. J. (2000). *God, The Oldest Question.* Chicago, IL: Loyola Press.

Radin, D. (2009). *Entangled Minds: Extrasensory Experiences in a Quantum Reality.* Kindle edition: Pocket Books.

Raichle, M. (2010). The Brain's Dark Energy. *Scientific American,* 7.

Rorty, E. b. (1992). *The Linguistic Turn, Essays in Philosophical Method.* Chicago, IL: University of Chicago Press.

Sabom, M. (1998). *Light and Death, One Doctor's Fascinating Account of Near-Death Experiences.* Grand Rapids, MI: Zondervan Publising House.

Schwartz, J. M. (2000). *The Mind & The Brain, Neuroplasiticity and the Power of Mental Force.* New York, NY: Harper Collins.

Shermer, M. (2011). *The Believing Brain.* New York, NY: Times Books: Henry Holt and Company, LLC.

Shushan, G. P. (2011). *Conceptions of the Afterlife in Early Civilizations: Universalism, Constructivism and Near-Death Experience* . London, England - New York, NY: Continuum International Publishing Group.

Thurman, R. A. (1994). *The Tibetan Book of the Dead.* New York, NY: Bantam Books.

Tolle, E. (2005). *A New Earth - Awakening to your life's purpose.* New York, NY: Penguin Group.

Van Lommel, P. (2007, April 3). *International Association of Near Death Experiences.* Retrieved May 5, 2010, 2010, from www.iands.org: www.iands.org

Wilson, T. (2003). *Strangers to Ourselves, discovering the Adaptive unconscious.* Cambridge, MS: Harvard Press.

Wolf, F. A. (1981). *Taking the Quantum Leap.* New York, NY: Harper & Row .

End Notes

[1] Gerald Schoenewolf, Ph.D.

[2] Wikipedia

[3] I use NDE as an expedient, but the term Near Death Experience, is a misnomer in my opinion. It confuses the issue. (NDE's, as UCE's are events that will be discussed in great detail later.) But to offer a list of all the subcategories of UCE's in one book would make the whole process unmanageable. For the sake of expediency, I use the term NDE as an example or shorthand reference to the whole category of UCE's.

[4] People in Paul's time knew nothing of psychosomatic effects and many so-called miraculously cured illnesses were probably psychosomatic problems to begin with.

[5] There is nearly universal consensus in modern New Testament scholarship on a core group of authentic Pauline epistles whose authorship is rarely contested: Romans, 1 and 2 Corinthians, Galatians, Philippians, 1 Thessalonians, and Philemon. Several additional letters bearing Paul's name are disputed among scholars, namely Ephesians, Colossians, 2 Thessalonians, 1 and 2 Timothy, and Titus. Scholarly opinion is sharply divided on whether or not Colossians and 2 Thessalonians are genuine letters of Paul. The remaining four contested epistles-- Ephesians, as well as the three known as the Pastoral epistles-- have been labeled pseudepigraphical works by most critical scholars. (Wikipedia)

[6] International Association of Near Death Studies

[7] Max Karl Ernst Ludwig Planck, FRS was a German theoretical physicist whose work on quantum theory won him the Nobel Prize in Physics in 1918.

[8] Bengaluru, Jan 16 (IANS) Eight richest men in the world own the same wealth as the 3.6 billion people who make up the poorest half of humanity, said a study by Oxfam, an international confederation of 19 social organizations, on Monday. "Just eight men own the same wealth as the 3.6 billion people. None of them has earned his fortune through talent or hard work, but by inheritance or accumulation through industries prone to corruption and cronyism," claimed the study released ahead of the World Economic Forum annual meeting at Davos in Switzerland from Tuesday.

[9] an alleged psychic ability allowing a person to influence a physical system without physical interaction.[

[10] The modern double-slit experiment is a demonstration that light and matter can display characteristics of both classically defined waves and particles based on the design of the experiment.

[11] Of one substance

[12] The modern double-slit experiment is a demonstration that light and matter can display characteristics of both classically

defined waves and particles; moreover, it displays the fundamentally probabilistic nature of quantum mechanical phenomena. Wikipedia

[13] Wikipedia

[14] the science of the origin and development of the universe. Modern astronomy is dominated by the Big Bang theory, which brings together observational astronomy and particle physics.

[15] Sometimes used to refer to parapsychology, a field of study concerned with the investigation of paranormal and psychic phenomena which include telepathy, precognition, clairvoyance, psychokinesis, near-death experiences, reincarnation, apparitional experiences, and other paranormal claims. It is often identified as pseudoscience

[16] Brain waves flat-lined

[17] Using what we know about the quantum level of the universe as a valid source of information.

[18] Newton's laws with Einstein's additions.

[19] the branch of metaphysics dealing with the nature of being.

[20] the branch of metaphysics dealing with the nature of being.

[21] the theory of knowledge, especially about its methods, validity, and scope.

[22] EEG - Electroencephalography is an electrophysiological monitoring method to record electrical activity of the brain

[23] Source: Kevin Williams at https://plus.google.com/115909310801492319518/posts

[24] dependent origination, or dependent arising, states that all things arise in dependence upon other things: "if this exists, that exists; if this ceases to exist, that also ceases to exist."

[25] Bernard d'Espagnat was a French theoretical physicist, philosopher of science, and author, best known for his work on the nature of reality.

[26] Information-theoretic death is loss of information within a brain to such an extent that recovery of the original person becomes theoretically impossible.

[27] Intersubjectivity is a term used in philosophy, psychology, sociology, and anthropology to represent the psychological relation between people. It is usually used in contrast to solipsistic individual experience, emphasizing our inherently social being.

[28] Although Buddhist teachings on the process of dying are somewhat confirmed by new scientific theories, the issue of re-incarnation is still an obstacle for most Westerners.

[29] Non-reductive primitive is a substance that cannot be reduced beyond its current state. For instance, matter and energy.

[30] To be clear, this is not an argument for or against the concept of reincarnation. But rather an illustration that some ancient civilizations have recognized that death is a process and not just an event.

[31] Wikipedia

[32] This article was published in two parts in Cryonics magazine, January and April 1994. A more highly annotated version can be found on Ralph Merkle's Cryonics Pages. See also cryobiologist Dr. Gregory Fahy's critique of this paper and Dr. Merkle's response. For an alternative repair scenario contributed by an anonymous biologist that circumvents Dr. Fahy's concerns, see "Realistic Scenario for Nanotechnological Repair of the Frozen Human Brain".

[33] Autolysis is the digestion of cells by their own enzymes.

[34] It is possible that these reports are accurate but the explanations are based on misinterpretations. Explanations are culturally based. Consequently, many unexplained phenomena are described with metaphors familiar to those resident in that culture.

[35] According to the Copenhagen interpretation, physical systems generally do not have definite properties prior to being measured, and quantum mechanics can only predict the probabilities that measurements will produce certain results. The act of measurement affects the system, causing the set of probabilities to reduce to only one of the possible values immediately after the measurement.

[36] Sometimes referred to as Zoroaster was a Persian; born between the eighteenth and sixth century BCE) and was an Iranian prophet and philosopher.

[37] a secondary phenomenon that occurs

[38] Sir John Carew Eccles, was an Australian neurophysiologist who won the 1963 Nobel Prize in physiology or medicine for his work on the synapse.

[39] Wikipedia

[40] I would call this monistic interactionism.

[41] Recall the example of the meta-structural pyramid at the beginning of this book.

[42] Qualia is a property of something (e.g., its feel or appearance, rather than the thing itself).

[43] Henry Pierce Stapp (born March 23, 1928 in Cleveland, Ohio) is an American **mathematical physicist,** known for his work in **quantum mechanics,** particularly the development of axiomatic **S-matrix theory,** the proofs of strong nonlocality properties, and the place of free will in the "orthodox" quantum mechanics of John von Neumann.[2]

[44] Henry Stapp is a quantum physicist who worked with both Wolfgang Pauli and Werner Heisenberg. In his 2004 book Mind, Matter, and Quantum

Theory, he develops a psychophysical theory of mind that depends on our modern understanding of reality in the light of quantum mechanics.

[45] I use the adjective, original, to distinguish the original religious principles from the distortions of many modern beliefs.

[46] C. G. Jung, The Archetypes and the Collective Unconscious (London 1996) p. 43

[47] The Archetypes and The Collective Unconscious (Collected Works of C.G. Jung Vol.9 Part 1)
C. G. Jung (Author), R.F.C. Hull (Translator)

[48] the gross body is the material physical mortal body that eats, breathes, and moves (acts).

[49] the subtle body is the body of the mind and the vital energies, which keep the physical body alive

[50] According to the theory, the fundamental constituents of reality are strings of the Planck length (about 10^{-33} cm) that vibrate at resonant frequencies. Every string, in theory, has a unique resonance, or harmonic. Different harmonics determine different fundamental particles. The tension in a string is on the order of the Planck force(10^{44} newtons). The graviton (the proposed messenger particle of the gravitational force), for example, is predicted by the theory to be a string with wave amplitude zero.

[51] Quantum superposition refers to the quantum mechanical property, which states that all particles exist in not one state, but all possible states at once.

[52] Because we can experience only three dimensions plus time, it is difficult to even imagine eleven dimensions, let alone describe them without the aid of mathematics.

[53] Edward Witten (born August 26, 1951) is an American theoretical physicist with a focus on mathematical physics who is currently the Professor of Mathematical Physics at the Institute for Advanced Study. Witten is a leading researcher in superstring theory: a theory of quantum gravity, supersymmetric quantum field theories, and other areas of mathematical physics. He is regarded by some of his peers as one of the greatest living physicists, perhaps even a successor to Albert Einstein.

[54] "Confusingly, however, in the quantum world superposition can mean something different entirely. At the quantum scale, particles can also be thought of as waves. Particles can exist in different states, for example they can be in different positions, have different energies or be moving at different speeds. But because quantum mechanics is weird, instead of thinking about a particle being in one state or changing between a variety of states, particles are thought of as existing across all the possible states at the same time. It's a bit like lots of waves overlapping each other. This situation is known as a superposition of states. If you're thinking in terms of

particles, it means a particle can be in two places at once. This doesn't make intuitive sense but it's one of the weird realities of quantum physics. However, once a measurement of a particle is made, and for example its energy or position is known, the superposition is lost and now we have a particle in one known state." Physics.org

[55] Sir Roger Penrose OM FRS (born 8 August 1931) is an English mathematical physicist, mathematician and philosopher of science. He is the Emeritus Rouse Ball Professor of Mathematics at the Mathematical Institute of the University of Oxford, as well as an Emeritus Fellow of Wadham College.

[56] Our conscious observation is not the only way probability becomes reality. There are many theories in this regard. For purposes of this book we will stay with this one which is called the Copenhagen Interpretation.

[57] According to the Copenhagen interpretation, physical systems generally do not have definite properties prior to being measured, and quantum mechanics can only predict the probabilities that measurements will produce certain results. The act of measurement affects the system, causing the set of probabilities to reduce to only one of the possible values immediately after the measurement. This feature is known as <u>wavefunction collapse</u>.

[58] Space-time is a four-dimensional system consisting of three spatial coordinates and one for time, in which it is possible to locate events.

[59] (from Julian Barbour 1999) How the New Physics is Validating Near-Death Concepts by C. D. Rollins"

[60] Pim van Lommel is a new death experience researcher and cardiologist from the Netherlands.

[61] The Big Bang theory is the prevailing cosmological model for the universe from the earliest known periods through its subsequent large-scale evolution. If the known laws of physics are extrapolated to the highest density regime, the result is a singularity which is typically associated with the Big Bang. Everything in the universe was compressed into this density regime.

[62] Acupuncture is a component of the health care system of China that can be traced back at least 2,500 years. The general theory of acupuncture is based on the premise that there are patterns of energy flow (Qi) through the body that are essential for health. Disruptions of this flow are believed to be responsible for disease

[63] "Anita Moorjani (born Anita Shamdasani) is a *New York Times* best-selling author of the book *Dying to be Me,* speaker, and intercultural consultant for multinational corporations. In 2006, after suffering cancer for almost four years, Anita's organs started shutting down and she slipped into a deep **coma**. She was rushed to the hospital where she claims to have

crossed into the afterlife during what she considers a **Near Death Experience (NDE)**. Upon returning from her NDE, her body healed from the **end-stage lymphoma** within a matter of days and within months was completely cancer free." Wikipedia

[64] I use the word God as a marker. A term that represents an idea or a concept. I do not claim nor deny the existence of the individual entity commonly referred to as God.

[65] [1] Carhart-Harris, RL, Erritzoe D, Williams T, et alia. "Neural correlates of the psychedelic state determined by fMRI studies with psilocybin," Proc. Nat. Acad. Of Sciences 109, no. 6 (Feb 2012): 2138-2143.
[2] Palhano-Fontes F, Andrade KC, Tofoli LF, et alia. "The Psychedelic State Induced by Ayahuasca Modulates the Activity and Connectivity of the Default Mode Network," PLoS One (2015).
[3] Carhart-Harris, RL, Muthukumaraswamy S, Roseman L, et alia. "Neural correlates of the LSD experience revealed by multimodal neuroimaging." Proc. Nat. Acad. of Sciences (Mar 2016).

[66] Space-time is the union of space and time first articulated by relativity.

[67] Albert Einstein quotes (German born American Physicist who developed the special and general theories of relativity. Nobel Prize for Physics in 1921. 1879-1955)

[68] God and the Astronomers (New York: W. W. Norton, 1992), p. 107. (p. 116 in the '78 edition)

[69] Wikipedia

[70] Stuart Alan Kauffman (born September 28, 1939) is an American medical doctor, theoretical biologist, and complex systems researcher who studies the origin of life on Earth.

[71] Gaius Plinius Secundus (23 AD – August 25, 79 AD), better known as Pliny the Elder.

[72] Georges Henri Joseph Édouard Lemaître was a Belgian priest, astronomer and professor of physics at the Catholic University of Leuven.[1] He proposed the theory of the expansion of the universe, widely misattributed to Edwin Hubble.[2]

[73] "Jacques Derrida (July 15, 1930 – October 9, 2004) was a French philosopher, born in Algeria. He as best known for developing a form of semiotic analysis known as deconstruction, which he discussed in numerous texts, and developed in the context of phenomenology. He is one of the major figures associated with post and postmodern philosophy." Wikipedia

[74] John Stuart Mill (20 May 1806 – 8 May 1873) was a British philosopher, economist and civil servant. An influential contributor to social theory, political theory, and political economy, his conception of liberty justified the freedom of the individual in opposition to unlimited state control.

[75] A New Kind of Law Beyond Entailing Law: August 22, 2011 ... Ensemble Approach Can Yield Statistical Laws Beyond Entailing Laws. ... start of this post, no law entails the detailed ... Thus evolution is not entailed. ... By Stuart Kauffman: http://www.npr.org/blogs/13.7/2011/08/22/139848246/a-new-kind-of-law-beyond-entailing-law-the-ensemble-approach.

[76] Absolutism: a philosophical theory in which values such as truth or morality are absolute and not conditional upon human perception

[77] Relativism: the belief that concepts such as right and wrong, goodness and badness, or truth and falsehood are not absolute, but change from culture to culture and situation to situation.

[78] Naïve realism, also known as direct realism or common sense realism, is a philosophy of mind rooted in a theory of perception that claims that the senses provide us with direct awareness of the external world.

[79] Emil Johann Wiechert (1861 – 1928) was a German geophysicist.

[80] St Augustine is quoted as having said those famous words, but there is no reference to this in his writings. Maybe Martin Luther said it first and it was attributed to Augustine.; Others say it was the other way around.

[81] A Turing machine is a theoretical device that manipulates symbols on a strip of tape according to a table of rules. Despite its simplicity, a Turing machine can be adapted to simulate the logic of any computer algorithm, and is particularly useful in explaining the functions of a CPU inside a computer.

[82] The originator of this quote remains a mystery. It could have been Phillip Graham of the Washington Post or it may have been Alan Barth, who wrote the New Republic article that contained this phrase. Barth was a Washington Post editorial writer from 1943 to 1972.

[83] Scientific American: The Brain's Dark Energy by Marcus E. Raichle, M.D. February 17, 2010

[84] Linguistic distinctions are the way we artificially parse reality into manageable chunks of information with the use of words. They allow us to experience reality as though it were discontinuous and distinct. When, in fact, it is continuous and connected.

[85] Our cognitive models also contain other components of our sensory systems.

[86] Martin Heidegger (September 1889 – 26 May 1976) was a seminal thinker in the **Continental** tradition and philosophical **hermeneutics**, with a growing influence on **Analytic** philosophy.

[87] A cognitive map (also: mental map or mental model) is a type of mental representation which serves an individual to acquire, code, store, recall, and decode information about the relative locations and attributes of phenomena

in their everyday or metaphorical spatial environment. The concept was introduced by Edward Tolman in 1948.

[88] *Tolman E.C. (July 1948). "Cognitive maps in rats and men". Psychological Review* **55** *(4): 189– 208. doi:10.1037/h0061626.PMID 18870876.*

[89] A reduction mechanism would work to decrease something in size, number, extent, degree, or intensity. In this present usage it reduces sensory input to our central nervous system.

[90] Tactile: relating to or used for the sense of touch.

[91] Visceral: characterized by or showing basic emotions

[92] a property of something, e.g. its feel or appearance, rather than the thing itself

[93] http://microbiology.usgs.gov/geomicrobiology_arsenic.html

[94] https://www.sciencenews.org/article/gravity-waves-black-holes-verify-einsteins-prediction?mode=magazine&context=1778

[95] Max Planck (April 23, 1858 – October 4, 1947) was a German physicist. He is considered to be the founder of the quantum theory, and thus one of the most important physicists of the twentieth century. Planck was awarded the Nobel Prize in Physics in 1918.

[96] Gleiser, Marcello, website: NPR.org, Blog: Cosmos and Culture, 13.7 , June, 2010

[97] Thomas Samuel Kuhn (July 18, 1922 – June 17, 1996) was an American historian and philosopher of science whose controversial 1962 book The Structure of Scientific Revolutions was deeply influential in both academic and popular circles, introducing the term "paradigm shift", which has since become an English-language staple.

[98] Embodied - Philosophers, cognitive scientists and artificial intelligence researchers who study embodied cognition and the embodied mind believe that the nature of the human mind is largely determined by the form of the human body. They argue that all aspects of cognition, such as ideas, thoughts, concepts and categories are shaped by aspects of the body. These aspects include the perceptual system, the intuitions that underlie the ability to move, activities and interactions with our environment and the naive understanding of the world that is built into the body and the brain.

[99] Morris Berman (b. 1914), Canadian educator, author. The Reenchantment of the World, ch. 1, Cornell University Press (1981).

[100] © www.abarim-publications.com 2000–2011

[101] The Higgs boson is an elementary particle in the Standard Model of particle physics.

[102] A consistent system is one that contains no contradictions.

[103] Recursive systems involve the repeated application of a function to its own values.

---

[104] Friedrich Wilhelm Nietzsche (1844 – 1900) was a nineteenth century German philosopher, poet, composer, and classical philologist.
[105] The population in 2016 is over 7.4 billion and growing

CPSIA information can be obtained
at www.ICGtesting.com
Printed in the USA
FFOW03n0427210217
32631FF

9 781634 920285